RichThoughts
for Breakfast
Volume 4

Harold Herring

President of The Debt Free Army
& RichThoughts TV

www.HaroldHerring.com

Debt Free Army
PO Box 900000, Fort Worth, TX 76161

RichThoughts for Breakfast Volume 4
by Harold Herring

ISBN 978-0-9763668-4-3
Copyright © 2015 by the Debt Free Army
PO Box 900000, Fort Worth, TX 76161
817-222-0011
harold@haroldherring.com

Unless otherwise noted, Scripture references are taken from the King James Version of the Bible.

Please obtain consent of the Author prior to any reproduction, whether in whole or in part, in any form.

Printed in the United States of America.
All rights reserved.

RichThoughts for Breakfast
Volume 4

Table of Contents

Day	Title	Page
1	7 Steps to Increase	7
2	7 Reasons To Get a Plan or Plan to Tread Water	15
3	You've Got More Than You Can See	25
4	7 Ways to Cheer Up Your Thought Life	33
5	10 Commandments of Success	41
6	7 Ways to Know If You're Really Alive	51
7	3 Guaranteed Ways to Improve Your Future	59
8	Whatcha Doing – Which of the 6 Are You?	67
9	5 Hindrances to Your Surplus	75
10	Avoiding Spiritual Icebergs	83
11	6 Things to Know If You Want God to Be Good to You	91
12	7 Reasons Why You Give To Get	99
13	How You Can Lack Nothing	107
14	Answering the Right Question Meets Every Need	115
15	Joshua's 10 Success Secrets	123
16	How to Get What You Ask For	131
17	7 Ways to Avoid Being a Prodigal	139
18	Use It or Lose It	147
19	The Lost Art That Brings You Success	155
20	What To Do When You Don't Know What To Do	163
21	5 Ways To Get God's Help	171
22	What's Your Money Philosophy?	179
23	What It Takes To Be a VIP	187
24	God Won't Remember	195
25	7 Reasons to Be Faithful With What You've Got	203
26	The Question God Wants Us To Answer	211
27	7 Keys to an Immediate Breakthrough	219
28	4 Reasons To Read the Instruction Manual	227
29	7 Reasons You Are Somebody	235

7 Steps to Increase

Day 1

Make no mistake about it! **God is interested in your finances.**

If God was not interested in your money, then it would be ridiculous for 20 percent of the scriptures to deal with money, wealth, finances, property, lands, possessions, tithes and giving. And yet they do.

Scripture clearly shows us that God cares about us and actually desires and is happy for us to prosper.

Psalm 35:27 says:

> "... yea, let them say continually, Let the Lord be magnified, which hath pleasure in the prosperity of his servant."

3 John 2 says:

> "Beloved, I wish above all things that thou mayest prosper and be in health even as thy soul prospers."

It's more important than ever that God's children understand what He says about money.

God is not glorified when all our energies are put into keeping a roof over our heads and putting food on the table.

The Body of Christ must know how to bring increase into their lives, and here are seven steps to increase:

Step 1—Give Expecting To Receive

God gave His greatest gift with full expectation of receiving something in return.

God gave His precious Son, because He knew He would receive many multiplied sons and daughters.

John 3:16 says:

> *"For God so loved the world,* **that he gave** *his only begotten Son, that whosoever believeth in him should not perish, but have everlasting life."*

By understanding God's actions, **we can see that giving is the first step toward receiving God's abundance in our lives.**

We will never achieve prosperity by just knowing about it … **we must give. If we do the giving, we can expect to receive something in return.**

Galatians 6:7 says:

> "Be not deceived; God is not mocked, for whatsoever a man soweth, that shall he also reap."

2 Corinthians 9:10 in the New Living Translation says:

> *"For God is the one who provides seed for the farmer and then bread to eat. In the same way, he will provide and increase your resources and then produce a great harvest of generosity in you."*

He will *"… produce a great harvest of generosity in you."* Hallelujah!! That's what I'm talking about.

Step 2—Bank on God's Promises

Commercial banks often offer us something so we will put our money in their institution. But God offers us the best banking program ever.

2 Corinthians 9:6, 8-11 in The Living Bible says:

> *"… A farmer who plants just a few seeds will get only a small crop, but if he plants much, he will reap much.*
>
> *"God is able to make it up to you by giving you everything you need and more, so that there will not only be enough for your own needs,*

but plenty left over to give joyfully to others.

"The godly man gives generously to the poor. His goods deeds will be an honor to him forever.

"For God, who gives seed to the farmer to plant, and later on, good crops to harvest and eat, will give you more and more seed to plant and will make it grow so that you can give away more and more fruit from your harvest.

"Yes, God will give you much so that you can give away much ..."

Each time you give an offering, God will return it to you multiplied. Be expectant! Just as an earthly banker knows the world's secrets of abundance, you can literally bank on God and His promises.

Step 3—Choose Faith Over Fear

The only way the devil can stop you from receiving your God-ordained portion of wealth is by getting you to accept his lies about your ability to break through into abundance.

The enemy will try to make you so afraid of failure, you will give up your newfound liberty in giving. Satan will desperately attempt to convince you that giving is foolish. His tactics are to make you fearful about your future.

God doesn't want you to operate in fear, but in power (2 Timothy 1:7). Remember, God gives you power to get wealth.

Deuteronomy 8:18 says:

> *"But thou shalt remember the Lord thy God: for it is he that giveth thee power to get wealth."*

Step 4—Tithe and Give Offerings

Hopefully you are tithing and giving offerings in obedience to the Word of God. Tithing and giving offerings are necessary to experience the major spiritual breakthrough you desire in your finances. Both of these actions trigger different sets of promises from God.

Your tithe will open the windows of heaven.

Your offerings will allow God to pour out a blessing through those open windows.

2 Corinthians 1:20 says:

> *"For all the promises of God in him are yea, and in him Amen, unto the glory of God by us."*

God's promises, combined with your faithful giving, will become the basis for your financial prosperity.

Stand in faith, confidently expecting God's promises to be fulfilled in your life.

Don't let your circumstances make a difference in your giving.

There is a time coming ... hallelujah ... where you will no longer live in a financial wilderness.

Your desert will bloom like a beautiful garden. **It won't happen because I say so; it will happen because the Word of God says so.**

Step 5—Plant Your Seed to Glorify God

I hope the principles of biblical economics are firmly rooted in your mind and in your actions, because the Lord's method of increase goes against most of the world's thinking.

The world leads you to get all the money you can and hold onto it. However, God has a different way.

Proverbs 11:24-25 in the New Living Translation says:

> *"Give freely and become more wealthy; be stingy and lose everything. The generous will prosper; those who refresh others will themselves be refreshed."*

If you will now begin to sow your financial seed, you will soon be reaping an ever-increasing harvest.

Then you will have everything you need, with plenty left over to finance God's end-time harvest.

Step 6—Reap Your Harvest

The circumstances in your life may not show any sudden improvement. Your finances may still be short. Your bills may still be difficult to pay. You may not have such abundance that your every need and desire is fulfilled, but keep standing on God's Word.

The devil might say something like, "You gave that big offering last week, and you still don't have anything."

Learn to recognize the devil's lies and cast them from your mind. Don't give attention to anything that exalts itself against the knowledge of God. *These tactics are the only thing the devil can use to stop your pending financial harvest.*

Remember, **the Word of God guarantees your harvest.** You can trust God, knowing He will provide the harvest He has promised you.

Step 7—Sow Again From Every Harvest

As your financial harvest begins to manifest, be sure you identify it.

Don't begin to think that your job or your material investments are your source. Keep your eyes open. Watch for God's blessings.

Part of your continuing success depends upon your recognition that God is your source. God is the one who supplies everything you need. With every upward advance in your finances, learn to thank the Lord.

As long as you remember who your source is, you will never forget to plant more seed from your abundance. Continue to tithe and give offerings from all the income you receive. Keep planting after every harvest. You must continue to plant seed if you desire to have a continual harvest.

Once you know God desires for you to prosper, you are in a position to receive His abundance through your faithful giving and receiving. If you are faithful to God, He will be faithful to you.

7 Reasons To Get a Plan or Plan to Tread Water

Years ago, I remember listening to an album by Bill Cosby.

One of the cuts on the album was "Noah." It was and still is really funny and clean.

There is one place in the routine where Cosby in his best God-like voice says, "Noah, can you tread water?"

My question for you is ... are you still treading water?

There was a time in our lives when we had one nostril above some mighty rough financially troubled waters, and every now and then we would have to gurgle just to keep from drowning in a sea of debt.

The reason Noah and his family didn't drown with everyone else on planet earth was because he had a goal, a plan and a willingness to make it happen in spite of the personal ridicule of neighbors who mocked them.

There are seven goal-setting steps to keep from

treading water.

1. **Your Goal Needs to Provide a Solution for Solving Your Problem.**

In Genesis 6:13 God told Noah the earth was filled with violence and evil, and that he was going to destroy everyone. God told Noah the problem and how he was going to solve it.

Are there problems you need to solve? What kind of goals do you need to set to solve your problems? I'm going to list the six major areas of life with a few general possibilities for your goal-setting agenda. You can use it to create your own specifics.

Spiritual ... daily Bible reading ... more time in prayer in your secret place ... getting involved in a full gospel church ...

Family ... quality time spent with your spouse and children ... date nights with your spouse ... instructing your children in the Word ...

Financial ... getting out of debt ... implementing creative ideas for new avenues of revenue ... planning for the future ... organizing your finances ... improving your skill set for a promotion at work or a new job altogether ...

Physical ... developing a regular exercise program ... eating healthier ... making lists with specific foods ... avoiding unhealthy and processed foods ...

Social ... participating in activities at church with your spouse and children ... attending school functions for your children or grandchildren ... interacting with other couples/singles ... individual activities with your children ...

Mental ... reading new books on a regular basis (weekly or monthly) ... listening to CDs that inspire and motivate you to greater levels of achievement in your life ... taking time to get away from your normal routine to refresh, relax and renew ...

2. Your Goals Must Be Specific.

If you don't have specific goals, you are just "wishing and a hoping." <u>Specificity greatly increases the likelihood of greater results</u>.

Genesis 6:14-15 in the New King James Version says:

> "Make yourself an **ark of gopherwood**; **make rooms** in the ark, and **cover it inside and outside with pitch**. And this is how you shall make it: The **length of the ark shall be three hundred cubits**, its **width fifty cubits**, and its **height thirty cubits**."

God also gave Noah the specifics on where to put the window, the door and how many decks to build.

Listed below are several examples of how to make goals specific.

Do you want a raise? How much? When do you want the raise to become effective?

When do you plan to pay off your first debt? How will you do it? What's your plan?

How much weight do you want to release? (I don't like the phrase "lose weight" because when you lose something … your natural reaction is to find it.) When will you start exercising? What days of the week? What exercises?

3. Your Goals Must Be Manageable and Measureable.

God gave Noah a very manageable plan on how to load the ark.

Genesis 6:19-21 in the New King James Version says:

> "And of every living thing of all flesh you shall bring two of every sort into the ark, to keep them alive with you; they shall be male and female. Of the birds after their kind, of animals after their kind, and of every creeping thing of the earth after its kind, two of every kind will come to you to keep them alive. And you shall take for yourself of all food that is eaten, and you shall gather it to yourself; and it shall be food for you and for them."

Your goals should not only be manageable; they

should be measureable as well.

1 Timothy 4:15 in the Amplified Bible says:

> "Practice and cultivate and meditate upon these duties; throw yourself wholly into them [as your ministry], so that your progress may be evident to everybody."

If you're serious about achieving your goals ... then you must be able to measure your progress.

4. You Must Have a Specific Timeline for Your Goals or You'll Tread Water.

In your planning remember that it doesn't matter if your goal has never been attempted or accomplished before.

In the Bill Cosby routine when God tells Noah that it's going to rain ... his response was: "Lord, what's rain?" It had never rained on planet earth up until that time.

If God inspires and directs your goals ... you will ALWAYS succeed.

Genesis 7:4 in the New King James Version says:

> "For after seven more days I will cause it to rain on the earth forty days and forty nights, and I will destroy from the face of the earth all living things that I have made."

5. You Must Complete Every Detail in Your Plans.

If there is one thing we can gather in reading these scriptures on Noah ... it's that God pays attention to the details.

When we follow His plan ... we will be commended for our obedience to His instructions.

Genesis 6:22 in the New King James Version says:

> *"Thus Noah did; according to all that God commanded him, so he did."*

In reading the story of Noah it becomes very clear that **God wants us to understand that Noah did what He was told to do.** God wants no less from each of us ... which is why a verse is repeated.

Genesis 7:5 in the New King James Version says:

> *"And Noah did according to all that the Lord commanded him."*

God might be a little impressed when we start goals ... but He is fully impressed when we complete them as He has directed.

6. Don't Be Concerned About What Others Think About Your Goals.

There will always be those who don't understand

your goals, or if they do, they are jealous and don't want you to succeed.

Can you imagine Noah's neighbors ... all the sinners laughing at a man who had a vision ... a specific direction from God?

Never be moved by what others think or say ... only by what God directs you to accomplish.

Remember this next statement.

Those who downplay, scoff at or ridicule your dreams will be left behind to suffer the consequences. If you doubt that ... think about Noah's neighbors.

7. You Will Be Rewarded for Accomplishing Your Goals.

Noah worshipped God with a significant offering, and God set into motion a blessing plan for generations to come.

Genesis 8:20-22 in the New King James Version says:

> *"Then Noah built an altar to the LORD, and took of every clean animal and of every clean bird, and offered burnt offerings on the altar. And the LORD smelled a soothing aroma. Then the LORD said in His heart, 'I will never again curse the ground for man's sake, although the imagination of man's heart is evil*

from his youth; nor will I again destroy every living thing as I have done.

" 'While the earth remains, seedtime and harvest, cold and heat, winter and summer, And day and night shall not cease.' "

It's time for you to get a plan for your life ... so you don't find yourself and those you love treading water.

Read how to personalize this for yourself in 1 Peter 2:24 in the Amplified Bible:

"He personally bore [Name's] *sins in His [own] body on the tree [as on an altar and offered Himself on it], that* [Name] *might die (cease to exist) to sin and live to righteousness. By His wounds* [Name] *has been healed."*

Before today ends, read Psalm 23 as your own personalized chapter. It will start like this:

"The Lord is my shepherd; [Name] shall not want.

"He maketh [Name] to lie down in green pastures: he leadeth [Name] beside the still waters.

"He restoreth [Name's] soul: he leadeth [Name] in the paths of righteousness for his name's sake ..."

Remember, **you will be rewarded for achieving your goals** ...

You've Got More Than You Can See

Some years ago when I was Director of Development for a Christian college in eastern North Carolina ... I went to see a successful farmer about a donation.

After giving the farmer a passionate message about investing into Christian education for the leaders of tomorrow ... he began to tell me that he had not had a good year financially. He claimed that the year was even worse than the year before.

I knew something about his financial situation, because his daughter attended the college where I was employed; and she was always talking about her Daddy.

For instance, I knew he'd purchased a new truck ($30K), a new Corvette for his wife ($40K), a new car for his daughter ($25K), a new tractor ($60K) and a new combine for harvesting his wheat ($70K) ... so I smiled and recited the lists of things that he'd paid cash for.

I will never forget how serious he was when he said, "Yes, I paid cash for all that stuff ... but I didn't have as much money left over to put in the bank as I did last year."

The success of his year was determined by how much money he had in the bank after he'd paid nearly $250,000 in cash for "stuff." So, in his mind, it had been a bad year.

What conditions have to exist for you to declare your situation to be bad?

For some ... it might be the reality of your home being foreclosed on because you are three months behind on the payments.

For others ... missing the payment on their Mercedes Benz ... would be a desperate situation.

The severity of the financial crisis depends upon your perspective ... or what you are, in fact, experiencing at the moment.

If there was a single woman in your church, and you discovered she and her son were down to their last meal ... would you consider that a desperate situation?

How do you view your own unmet needs?

Regardless, **the real question is how does God view our situation?**

1 Kings 17:12 says:

> "And she said, As the LORD thy God liveth, I have not a cake, but an handful of meal in a barrel, and a little oil in a cruse: and, behold, I am gathering two sticks, that I may go in and dress it for me and my son, <u>that we may eat it, and die</u>."

God sent the prophet to see this widow at Zarephath. A lesser man of God may have wondered what God was up to when he saw how poor this woman was ... but **Elijah knew God wouldn't have sent him there if He hadn't had a plan.**

When the widow looked around, she thought she was going to die.

The scripture indicates that God had given her an instruction leading to hope, but from her words to Elijah, she had despaired of her answer coming.

Have you ever felt that way?

Child of God, you are about to discover something very powerful in 1 Kings 17:9 which says:

> "Arise, get thee to Zarephath, which belongeth to Zidon, and dwell there: behold, I have **<u>commanded a widow woman there to sustain thee</u>**."

In the natural, it did not appear that this woman could

be the one called to sustain the prophet.

The Amplified Bible says: *"... I have commanded a widow there to provide for you."*

The New Living Translation says: *"... I have instructed a widow there to feed you."*

The New Century Version says: *"... I have commanded a widow there to take care of you."*

Are you getting this?

Here's a woman who thinks she is about to have her last meal with her son and then die. **The "circumstances" were undoubtedly very real to her**. But the "truth" recorded in the Word of God said her purpose was to "sustain," "provide for," "feed" and "take care" of the prophet.

God saw something in her finances that she did not see.

Wow ... thank you Lord ... that's such a Rich Thought.

I want you to write this down.

God sees something in my finances today that I do not see ... yet.

God sees something in my finances today that I do not see ... yet.

The widow didn't see what God was about to do in her finances.

Truthfully, it was probably something Elijah didn't see with the natural eye either but accepted by faith and the direction of the Lord, for 1 Kings 17:13 says:

> *"And Elijah said unto her, Fear not; go and do as thou hast said: but make me thereof a little cake first, and bring it unto me, and after make for thee and for thy son."*

The prophet gave the widow very specific instructions in this verse. He said:

1. Fear not.

No doubt the widow was thinking ... that's easy for you to say ... you're not the one dying here.

2. Go.

Don't just stand around talking ... do what God says to do!

3. Do.

<u>Way too many believers spend way too much time talking about what they're going to do instead of just doing it</u>.

4. Make me a cake FIRST.

How would you react if you were down to your last meal, and the man of God said, "Stop! Make me a meal first before you feed yourself and your son."?

5. Bring it to me.

Not only did the prophet want her last cake ... he had the nerve to tell her to bring it to him.

6. Make a cake for you and your son.

Then he gives her permission to do something for herself and her son. That is, after she's taken care of the prophet ... waiting on him hand and foot ... giving him water and then what she thought was her last meal ... he now tells her she can make a cake for herself.

This widow woman faced many obstacles that could have made her doubt what the man of God said, but she obeyed his instructions anyway.

You may think you're at the end ... with nowhere to turn ... but I doubt that anyone hearing my voice this morning has faced the prospect of one last meal with your child before dying. She was not in a position to beg from others, because no one else had anything either due to the famine.

This widow woman had a choice ... in the direst of circumstances, she looked beyond her situation and acted in faith on the word given to her by the man of God.

As a result of that obedience the widow woman was told the following in 1 Kings 17:14 in the New Living Translation which says:

> "... There will always be flour and olive oil left in your containers until the time when the Lord sends rain and the crops grow again!"

If she had not responded "in faith" on "the Word," things could have easily been different. **There is a spirit of poverty and lack that makes you want to hold onto what you have in fear of that being all there is.**

There are some people who are so fearful about getting down to their last dollar that they squeeze George Washington until he begins to cry.

Here's what the Lord is stirring in me ... **hold on too tightly to what you have, and you'll lose it.**

You need to understand how God views your finances and then obey His directions. You find them in the Book!

No matter what's in your bank account ... you must always remember that you've got more than you can see.

Remember what I had you write down earlier in this teaching.

God sees something in your finances that you do

not see ... yet.

I posted on Facebook this morning:

"God is doing more for you right now ... that you can't see ... so He can bring into manifestation ... the things you can see."

7 Ways to Cheer Up Your Thought Life

The Word says I don't have to worry about anything as long as I pray about everything.

Philippians 4:6 in the New Living Translation says:

> *"Don't worry about anything; instead, pray about everything. Tell God what you need, and thank him for all he has done."*

If you're facing problems ... dealing with worries ... you need Someone who can cheer you up.

Psalm 94:18-19 in the Amplified Bible says:

> *"When I said, My foot is slipping, Your mercy and loving-kindness, O Lord, held me up. In the multitude of my [anxious] thoughts within me, Your comforts cheer and delight my soul!"*

The New Living Translation of Psalm 94:18-19 says:

> *"I cried out, 'I am slipping!' but your unfailing love, O Lord, supported me. When doubts*

filled my mind, your comfort gave me renewed hope and cheer."

When you're dealing with worry, doubt and fear ... why would you ever turn to anyone other than the Lord ... who not only listens to your problems but offers solutions from His Word. It only requires looking to and leaning on Him.

If you're going through a rough patch in your life ... isn't it comforting to know that your loving Heavenly Father will hold you up and support you?

If you can fog a mirror ... if you're drawing a breath right now ... the enemy will seek on a regular basis to fill your mind with doubts.

Just because the devil sends thoughts your way doesn't mean that you have to receive or accept them.

When the enemy wants you to doubt whether you'll ever get out of debt or have enough money to pay your bills on time ... remind him of what the Word says.

When the enemy wants you to doubt whether the pains you're feeling right now or the sickness in your body will ever go away ... remind him of what the Word says.

When the enemy wants you to doubt whether your children will ever serve the Lord the way they did when they were young ... remind him of what the Word says.

There is one thing that you can always count on with the enemy ... he will hijack your thought process unless you stop Him.

Just for the record ... **God knows everything you're thinking, and He wants you to cheer up your thought life.**

Here are seven ways you can do ... exactly that.

1. God is thinking about you RIGHT NOW.

Jeremiah 29:11 says:

> "For I know the thoughts that I think toward you, saith the LORD, thoughts of peace, and not of evil, to give you an expected end."

We need to get this ... God is thinking about US. In fact, God is thinking about YOU.

You may have felt that nobody knew you were alive, including your family ... but that's just not true ... because God, your Heavenly Father, is thinking about you.

Psalm 40:17 in The Living Bible says:

> "I am poor and weak, yet the Lord is thinking about me right now! ..."

I want you to write down the last part of Psalm 40:17.

> "... the Lord is thinking about me right now."

Personalize it.

> "... the Lord is thinking about [Name] right now."

2. God knows what sinners are thinking and gives them a way of escape.

Matthew 9:4 in the New Living Translation says:

> "Jesus knew what they were thinking, so he asked them, 'Why do you have such evil thoughts in your hearts?' "

Matthew 6:32 in the New Living Translation says:

> "These things dominate the thoughts of unbelievers, but your heavenly Father already knows all your needs."

What's the greatest need of a sinner ... salvation.

1 John 1:9 says:

> "If we confess our sins, he is faithful and just to forgive us our sins, and to cleanse us from all unrighteousness."

3. You cannot put positive thoughts and

negative thoughts into the same environment and expect success.

If you're putting the Word of God into your mental thought process, but you're also mentally entertaining negative, ungodly thoughts, then you might survive, but it will be difficult for you to thrive.

James 1:8 says:

> "A double minded man is unstable in all his ways."

Luke 11:17 in the New Living Translation says:

> "He knew their thoughts, so he said, 'Any kingdom divided by civil war is doomed. A family splintered by feuding will fall apart.'"

F. F. Bosworth, the author of *Christ the Healer,* said:

"Faith and doubt cannot live in the same house."

4. Refocus your thinking on God's Word and His solutions to your every problem.

Romans 12:2 in the New Living Translation says:

> "Don't copy the behavior and customs of this world, but let God transform you into a new person by changing the way you think. Then

you will learn to know God's will for you, which is good and pleasing and perfect."

Isaiah 26:3 also in the New Living Translation says:

"You will keep in perfect peace all who trust in you, all whose thoughts are fixed on you!"

5. Make sure your thoughts are well-pleasing to Him.

Psalm 104:34 in the New Living Translation says:

"May all my thoughts be pleasing to him, for I rejoice in the Lord."

Psalm 19:14 says:

"Let the words of my mouth, and the meditation of my heart, be acceptable in thy sight, O LORD, my strength, and my redeemer."

6. The only effective way to change your life is by changing your thoughts and attitudes.

Isaiah 28:9, 10 says:

"Whom shall he teach knowledge? … For precept must be upon precept, precept upon precept; line upon line, line upon line; here a little, and there a little."

Ephesians 4:23 in the New Living Translation says:

> "Instead, let the Spirit renew your thoughts and attitudes."

7. Let His thoughts be your thoughts.

Psalm 51:10 says:

> "Create in me a clean heart, O God; and renew a right spirit within me."

Joshua 1:8 gives us the key to a successful thought life and is the only time in the King James Version where the word "success" is used:

> "This book of the law shall not depart out of thy mouth; but thou shalt meditate therein day and night, that thou mayest observe to do according to all that is written therein: for then thou shalt make thy way prosperous, and then thou shalt have good success."

The Word says that we have the mind of Christ ... so it's time to let His thoughts become our thoughts.

Isaiah 55:8-9 is often misinterpreted as a scripture that says we can never know God's thoughts, but let's look at it more closely:

> "For My thoughts are not your thoughts, neither are your ways My ways, says the Lord. For as the heavens are higher than the earth,

so are My ways higher than your ways and My thoughts than your thoughts."

God is making a declaration that He is not only above but far above our thought process.

God would not be constantly reaching out for man if He did not want us to come up to His way of thinking. Understand this exactly how I said it. God is saying His thoughts are above ours. Too often Christians want to bring God's thoughts down to where we are.

God wants to bring our thought life up to His level.

And 1 Corinthians 2:16 declares:

> *"For who hath known the mind of the Lord, that he may instruct him? but we have the mind of Christ."*

If you need cheering up ... if you need to be comforted ... spend your time with the One who is thinking in a positive way about you.

Can somebody say "Hallelujah."

10 Commandments of Success

I came across *The Ten Commandments of Success* written by Charles M. Schwab, the steel magnate in the early 20th Century.

Based on his lifestyle, I find it ironic that Schwab chose the term "commandments" to describe his success strategies. His lifestyle was anything but that of a godly man. Yet, back in that day, doing the godly thing was more the norm in American life than in today's society.

Schwab was a brilliant businessman. In 1908, he took a major risk and had his company, Bethlehem Steel, begin construction of the H-beam, which revolutionized building construction and made possible the age of the skyscraper.

As I read Schwab's ten commandments of success ... I was stirred to give them a scriptural foundation and a few comments.

After all, each of these commandments has scripture as its basis. For that matter, **all success is born in**

scripture. It just isn't always recognized as such.

Let's take a *Godly* (as God sees it) look at Schwab's ten commandments of success.

1. Work hard. Hard work is the best investment a man can make.

Ezra 5:8 in the New Living Translation says:

> "The king should know that we went to the construction site of the Temple of the great God in the province of Judah. It is being rebuilt with specially prepared stones, and timber is being laid in its walls. The work is going forward with great energy and success."

Here's a question ... are you working with great energy on your job ... if so, you will no doubt be a success.

Proverbs 14:23 in the New International Version says:

> "All hard work brings a profit, but mere talk leads only to poverty."

2. Study hard. Knowledge enables a man to work more intelligently and effectively.

1 Thessalonians 4:11 says:

> "And that ye study to be quiet, and to do your own business, and to work with your own hands, as we commanded you."

2 Timothy 2:15 says:

> "Study to shew thyself approved unto God, a workman that needeth not to be ashamed, rightly dividing the word of truth."

You may never have had your parents' approval in life ... but you can truly have your Heavenly Father's approval.

3. Have initiative. Ruts often deepen into graves.

Years ago, I saw a cross-stitched saying that stirred me then even as it still does today.

"Initiative is doing the right thing without being told to do it."

Matthew 7:12 in the Message Bible says:

> "Here is a simple, rule-of-thumb guide for behavior: Ask yourself what you want people to do for you, then grab the initiative and do it for them. Add up God's Law and Prophets and this is what you get."

4. Love your work. Then you will find pleasure in mastering it.

Ecclesiastes 3:22 in the Contemporary English Version says:

> "We were meant to enjoy our work, and that's the best thing we can do. We can never know the future."

If you hate your job ... it will show in your work ethics and your facial expressions. However, if you love your job ... it will also show in your expressions and your work ethics.

5. Be exact. Slipshod methods bring slipshod results.

Genesis 27:8 in the New Living Translation says:

> "Now, my son, listen to me. Do exactly as I tell you."

Exodus 25:9 in the New Living Translation says:

> "You must build this Tabernacle and its furnishings exactly according to the pattern I will show you."

Anything less than excellence ... is not acceptable to God.

6. Have the spirit of conquest. Thus you can successfully battle and overcome difficulties.

Isaiah 41:10 in the Amplified Bible says:

> "Fear not [there is nothing to fear], for I am with you; do not look around you in terror and be dismayed, for I am your God.
>
> "I will strengthen and harden you to difficulties, yes, I will help you; yes, I will hold you up and retain you with My [victorious] right hand of rightness and justice."

Romans 8:37 in the Amplified Bible says:

> "Yet amid all these things we are more than conquerors and gain a surpassing victory through Him Who loved us."

Read "7 Steps to Become a Kingdom Conqueror and World Overcomer" at haroldherring.com to learn more about this outstanding and spirit-building truth.

7. Cultivate personality. Personality is to a man what perfume is to a flower.

Proverbs 20:27 in the Amplified Bible says:

> "The spirit of man [that factor in human personality which proceeds immediately from God] is the lamp of the Lord, searching all his innermost parts."

Ephesians 3:16 in the Amplified Bible says:

> "May He grant you out of the rich treasury of His glory to be strengthened and reinforced with mighty power in the inner man by the [Holy] Spirit [Himself indwelling your innermost being and personality]."

1 Timothy 4:16 in the Amplified Bible says:

> "Look well to yourself [to your own personality] and to [your] teaching; persevere in these things [hold to them], for by so doing you will save both yourself and those who hear you."

8. Help and share with others. The real test of business greatness lies in giving opportunities to others.

Hebrews 13:16 in the Message Bible says:

> "Make sure you don't take things for granted and go slack in working for the common good; share what you have with others. God takes particular pleasure in acts of worship—a different kind of "sacrifice"—that take place in kitchen and workplace and on the streets."

Ephesians 6:8 in the Amplified Bible says:

> "Knowing that for whatever good anyone does, he will receive his reward from the Lord, whether he is slave or free."

When expectations are set high, it is so that we become better at what we do.

When we become better at what we do, we build a confidence in ourselves and with our peers.

When we have confidence we generate an aura ... and it becomes the aura of a winner.

The most important thing to remember is that a good business woman offers options every time to her clients.

She never assumes or judges what she thinks the customer will say; she does what an agent should do: She shows solutions and value.

9. Be democratic. Unless you feel right toward your fellow men, you can never be a successful leader of men.

Galatians 6:10 in the Amplified Bible says:

> *"So then, as occasion and opportunity open up to us, let us do good [morally] to all people [not only being useful or profitable to them, but also doing what is for their spiritual good and advantage]. Be mindful to be a blessing, especially to those of the household of faith [those who belong to God's family with you, the believers]."*

Luke 6:31 in the Amplified Bible says:

> "And as you would like and desire that men would do to you, do exactly so to them."

10. In all things do your best. The man who has done his best has done everything. The man who has done less than his best has done nothing.

Proverbs 21:31 in the Message Bible says:

> "Do your best, prepare for the worst—then trust God to bring victory."

Colossians 3:22 in the Message Bible says:

> "Servants, do what you're told by your earthly masters. And don't just do the minimum that will get you by. Do your best. Work from the heart for your real Master, for God, confident that you'll get paid in full when you come into your inheritance. Keep in mind always that the ultimate Master you're serving is Christ. The sullen servant who does shoddy work will be held responsible. Being a follower of Jesus doesn't cover up bad work."

Perhaps Charles Schwab's most famous quotation was:

"A man to carry on a successful business must

have imagination. He must see things as in a vision, a dream of the whole thing."

I like the way the Word says it in Romans 4:17 ... where God gives us the ability to *"... create new things out of nothing."*

The interesting thing about commandments, whether the ten that Moses brought down from the mountain or the ones penned by Charles Schwab ... **if you don't obey them ... you're not going to find the success you seek.**

According to Wikipedia.com, "Charles Schwab even before the Great Depression had already spent most of his fortune estimated at between $25 million and $40 million. Adjusted for inflation, that equates to between $500 million and $800 million in the first decade of the 21st century."

Wikipedia goes on to say that "Charles Schwab himself died bankrupt, living on borrowed money for five years before his death."

One last thing ... **success without God is temporary and fleeting even if you created a successful business empire and wrote The Ten Commandments of Success.**

7 Ways to Know If You're Really Alive

Day 6

I sat down at my desk to read and was lead to 1 Corinthians 15:20-22 which says:

> "But now is Christ risen from the dead, and become the firstfruits of them that slept.
>
> "For since by man came death, by man came also the resurrection of the dead. For as in Adam all die, **even so in Christ shall all be made alive.**"

I looked up the words *"... in Christ shall all be made alive"* in the Strong's Concordance.

The word "alive" is the Greek word ***zōopoieō*** (G2227) and it means:

> **"to cause to live; by spiritual power to arouse and invigorate; to give increase of life; or of seeds quickened into life, i.e. germinating, springing up, growing."**

As I read the definitions the Lord quickened several things in my spirit.

First, He wants you to *live*. There is more to living than just inhaling and exhaling oxygen, occupying space and going through the motions of a daily life.

God saved us for a purpose ... that purpose wasn't to look at today as just another day that the Lord has made. Yes, we are to have that viewpoint ... but so much more is involved in it.

Second, He clearly wants us to anticipate the dawn of a new day with expectancy. Greet each day with anticipation and expectation of what God is going to do in and through us.

God does not want us to settle for whatever and whoever comes our way.

The scripture in Luke 19:13 says we're to *"... occupy until I come."*

I looked up the word *occupy* in the Strong's Concordance ... it's ***pragmateuomai*** (G4231) and it means:

> **"to be occupied in anything; to carry on in business"** and **"to carry on the business of a banker or a trader."**

The word *occupy* also comes from the root of a Greek word **meaning "that which has been done, a deed, an accomplished fact"** or **"what is done or being accomplished."**

As I read those definitions in the concordance, it became even clearer ... **our Heavenly Father does not want us just sitting around biding our time waiting for Jesus to return.**

We should be more concerned about growing up in Jesus than going up to Him.

As the definition of *alive* says, **He wants us aroused and invigorated by His spiritual power working in and through us.**

He never wants us to experience rigor mortis of the mind or spirit to where our lives are hardened unto a death life or catatonic state.

God wants us *alive* and about His business of *occupying* wherever we are and whatever we're doing.

He has given us the power to get wealth (Deuteronomy 8:18) so that we can be a blessing to others.

We can't bless anybody else if we're broke, just getting by or hoping that the rapture will come before the first of the month since we don't have money to pay all the bills.

God wants us producing fruit in our lives ... manifesting the gifting and blessings of the Lord.

God wants us to greet each new day realizing that we have the opportunity to plant "seeds quickened into life, i.e. germinating, springing up, growing." **God**

wants us to attempt great things for Him.

Without question, God wants us to understand that *"the thief's purpose is to steal and kill and destroy ..."* (John 10:10)

However, I don't feel that God wants us focusing on the first part of that verse ... where the emphasis is on the attacks of the enemy. God wants you and me to grasp, manifest and make alive the last part of John 10:10 in our lives.

> *"... I am come that they might have life, and that they might have it more abundantly."*

The last part of John 10:10 in the New Living Translation says:

> *"... My purpose is to give them a rich and satisfying life."*

The last part of John 10:10 in the Amplified Bible says:

> *"... I came that they may have and enjoy life, and have it in abundance (to the full, till it overflows)."*

Personalize these verses by putting your name in them ... (I've done the first one for you.)

> *"... I am come that [Name] might have life, and that [he/she] might have it more abundantly."*

When you and I become alive in Christ ... we realize that we "might" have life ... that was our first choice and that we "might" have it more abundantly ... that's another choice.

In order to have life and experience it more abundantly ... we must be ALIVE in Him occupying until He comes again. We must be about His business ... which is also the business of the world.

We're the ones ... who should be controlling the financial markets, the banking system and the businesses of this country and the world.

If you don't feel prepared to assume this scriptural mantle, then PREPARE yourself.

Remember, the New Living Translation of John 10:10 says:

> "... My purpose is to give them a rich and satisfying life."

You can't enjoy the rich and satisfying life He has in mind for us ... by just going along ... to get along ... so you can just get by. That's not what being "alive" means to your Lord and Savior.

Here are seven things God expects of those who are really alive.

1. Remain mentally alert.

Jeremiah 1:12 in the Amplified Bible says:

> "Then said the Lord to me, You have seen well, for I am alert and active, watching over My word to perform it."

Now listen to Jeremiah 1:12 in the Message Bible which will make you shout.

> "And God said, 'Good eyes! I'm sticking with you. I'll make every word I give you come true.'"

2. Occupy until He comes.

Luke 19:13 in the New Living Translation says:

> "Before he left, he called together ten of his servants and divided among them ten pounds of silver, saying, 'Invest this for me while I am gone.'"

Occupying obviously means much more than just taking up space waiting for the rapture.

3. Maximize the spiritual and personal power working in us.

Ephesians 3:20 in the New Living Translation says:

> "Now all glory to God, who is able, through <u>his mighty power at work within us, to accomplish infinitely more than we might ask or think</u>."

4. Create opportunities instead of settling for what's available.

Colossians 4:5 in the New English Translation says:

> "Conduct yourselves with wisdom toward outsiders, making the most of the opportunities."

If we're not looking for opportunities for God to be glorified in and through our lives ... we will not recognize them when they present themselves.

5. Attempt great things for Him.

On May 30, 1792, William Carey, known as the father of modern missions, made a profound statement at the Baptist Association Meeting in Northampton, England, when he said:

> **"Expect great things; attempt great things."**

Ephesians 1:19 in the Amplified Bible says:

> "And [so that you can know and understand] what is the immeasurable and unlimited and surpassing greatness of His power in and for us who believe, as demonstrated in the working of His mighty strength."

6. Assume a position of leadership in our environment.

Exodus 18:20 in the Message Bible says:

> "Your job is to teach them the rules and instructions, to show them how to live, what to do."

In order to be successful in life you must have a successor ... which means **you must train those who work with you** to effectively handle the things you need help in achieving.

7. Invigorate ourselves afresh for every new day.

Colossians 1:11 in the Amplified Bible says:

> "[We pray] that you may be _invigorated_ and strengthened with all power according to the might of His glory, [to exercise] every kind of endurance and patience (perseverance and forbearance) with joy."

So here's the question ... are you alive with spiritual power invigorating every new day that He gives you?

3 Guaranteed Ways to Improve Your Future

I'm smiling as I say that I was led to a scripture about you. That's right, a scripture about everyone reading this right now.

Proverbs 9:9 in the New Living Translation says:

> *"Instruct the wise, and they will be even wiser. Teach the righteous, and they will learn even more."*

I know you're wise because you made the effort to open this book.

I'm not saying that out of a prejudiced perspective but rather the simple truth ... it's obvious you're seeking more information, revelation and motivation on your journey to financial independence.

My motivation is aptly described in Proverbs 9:9 in the Message Bible:

> *"Save your breath for the wise—they'll be wiser for it; tell good people what you know—they'll profit from it."*

My desire is for you to profit from what God has allowed me to see and experience personally or read and learn from others.

My desire is for you to maximize your potential and performance for Kingdom Living.

I also know beyond a shadow of a doubt that if you don't like where you are in life right now ... chances are there's something you don't know yet.

Regardless of your education or lack thereof ... background or experience ... you can move from where you are ... to where God wants you to be by following these three simple rules.

First, if you purpose in your heart to read at least one hour a day ... you will be able to read a book a week.

Of course, I'm not talking about books the size of *War and Peace* ... but the size of an average book sold today.

To deal with any who may doubt what I've just said ... let's say that it takes you two weeks at an hour a day to read a book. By following such a schedule you will still read 26 books in a year.

How many books did you read last year?

According to an Associated Press poll ... over 27% of Americans did not read a single book last year. Half of the people surveyed read four books or less last year. The survey also revealed that over 25% of those surveyed had read 15 books or more.

When you read a book every two weeks, or 26 per year, that number will put you in the upper 25% of all people in the United States. Think about your preparation for a job compared to others for a few minutes.

Here's another fact: If you read an hour a day about something you know nothing about ... within a year ... you will be an expert in your community. Within three years, you will be an expert in your state. Within five years, you will be internationally recognized in your field.

If you are currently unemployed, then truthfully you should spend even more time reading ... learning ... preparing. It's like sowing seed for a much richer future.

There are certain industries where things will never again be like they were before. There is a paradigm shift taking place in the 21st century workforce, and you must be prepared for the future or you will be left behind. But more about this later in this teaching.

A word of warning for those who say they don't like to read.

First, **STOP IT**.

Don't say that anymore ... every time you utter those

words you are empowering ignorance and more attacks of the enemy.

Second, it you don't like to read, then you need to get a pair of scissors and cut out several verses of scripture. The first is 2 Timothy 2:15 in the Amplified Bible:

> "Study and be eager and do your utmost to present yourself to God approved (tested by trial), a workman who has no cause to be ashamed, correctly analyzing and accurately dividing [rightly handling and skillfully teaching] the Word of Truth."

If you're going to study ... it means you have to READ. So, if you don't read, how can you study? And if you don't study, then you're disobeying a direct instruction from the Word of God.

Revelation 1:3 says:

> "Blessed is he that readeth, and they that hear the words of this prophecy, and keep those things which are written therein: for the time is at hand."

If you want to be blessed, you will be a reader ... if you want to obey God's command to study ... then you will be a reader.

One last point ... if you want to know more about finances, read financial books. If you want to know more about healing ... read words of wisdom on healing.

Heed the words of 1 Timothy 4:15 in the Message Bible:

> "Cultivate these things. Immerse yourself in them. The people will all see you mature right before their eyes! Keep a firm grasp on both your character and your teaching. Don't be diverted. Just keep at it. Both you and those who hear you will experience salvation."

Second, secure a "University on Wheels" degree.

If you're serious about your future success, then minimize sports or political talk radio or the music stations ... listen to teaching CDs instead.

Listen to your pastor's sermon from last Sunday, professional development teaching series or any of the absolutely fantastic teaching CDs from the Debt Free Army (smiling). Educate and empower yourself while you drive.

If you commute more than 30 minutes a day ... five days a week ... whether it's to work or on errands ... that's 150 minutes a week ... 7,800 minutes a year or a total of 130 hours per year in your daily drive ... which equals over 16 work days a year.

Think of your future when you are putting that much new and exciting knowledge into your mind each year.

Now let's look at this from a little different perspective. If you take 130 hours a year ... that would translate into three college courses with three credit hours each. Now consider the fact that the average person spends 500 hours in the car ... that would equal two semesters with a full load.

In other words, in four years based on the average time a person spends in a car, you would have the equivalent learning experience of two semesters or one year of a university education.

Finally, the jobs and the times ... they are a changing ... is more than the lyrics of a Bob Dylan song.

The top ten jobs in demand in 2012 did not exist in 2004.

According to the United States Department of Labor, the average learner today will have 10-14 different jobs by the time he or she is 38.

The amount of new technical information is doubling every two years. For students seeking a four-year technical degree ... that means that half of the information they've learned will be outdated by their third year of study.

If you're unemployed or desiring a new career field ... invest your time in a field of study at your local community college. Even in the changing workplace environment you must be in a state of continuing education.

Don't get snagged by some of the technical colleges that have high tuitions but offer easy student loans with deferred high interest rates. Your tax dollars pay for community colleges, so take advantage of the opportunities they afford. They are much less expensive and work hard to help working people.

You can also choose to increase your skills through FREE materials available on the Internet.

Bottom line, **plan your future ... and be a learner.**

Let me close this teaching with a powerful quote and a scripture.

Author and speaker Reid Buckley said:

"If you are not continually learning and upgrading your skills ... somewhere, someone else is, and when you meet that person in the competitive marketplace, you will lose."

The Word of God in Proverbs 9:11-12 in the New Living Translation says:

> *"Wisdom will multiply your days and add years to your life. If you become wise, you will be the one to benefit. If you scorn wisdom, you will be the one to suffer."*

Whatcha Doing – Which of the 6 Are You?

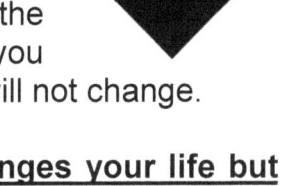

I have a revelation for you ... if you hear a great sermon every day of the year ... but do not act on what you hear, then the quality of your life will not change.

It's not what you hear that changes your life but rather what you do with what you hear.

James 1:23 in the Amplified Bible says:

> *"For if anyone only listens to the Word without obeying it and being a doer of it, he is like a man who looks carefully at his [own] natural face in a mirror."*

The Message Bible Translation of James 1:24 says:

> *"Those who hear and don't act are like those who glance in the mirror, walk away, and two minutes later have no idea who they are, what they look like."*

Bottom line ... **the only way to retain what you've heard is to do something with it.**

For most of my life I've heard preacher after preacher admonish his congregation or listeners to be a doer of the Word and not just a hearer.

The most frequently quoted scripture on being a doer of the Word is James 1:22 which says:

> "But be ye doers of the word, and not hearers only, deceiving your own selves."

The New Living Translation of James 1:22 says:

> "But don't just listen to God's word. You must do what it says. Otherwise, you are only fooling yourselves."

In other words, **if we're not doing the Word ... then we're deceiving or fooling ourselves.** Not only that, but if we're not doing what we heard ... we'll never retain what we've heard regardless of the revelation. Everything will go in one ear and out the other.

I find it interesting that the last part of the verse says we are deceiving or fooling ourselves.

There is an old saying that the biggest fool is the one who fools himself.

Make no mistake ... God wants you hearing the Word ... but He also wants you doing something with what you've heard.

According to Strong's Concordance *doer* is the Greek

word ***poiētēs*** (G4152) and it means:

"a maker, a producer, author, doer, performer."

In essence, you are the writer, actor, producer and director of your own life ... what you do ... how the script of your life plays out ... is entirely in your hands based on what you choose to do or not to do.

I think it's also important to point out that there are six different kinds of doers.

First, there is the PRETEND DOER ...

Someone who pretends to be a Christian ... pretends to be a tither ... pretends to love God with all their heart.

The motivation of the Pretender varies based on what's really in his or her heart.

You can Pretend to love God with all your heart ... you can Pretend that you're sold out and radical, but if you spend your time ... surfing the internet for porn or living a fantasy life filled with immoral thoughts ... then you're just the Great Pretender.

Second, there is the SELECTIVE DOER ...

The selective doer will pick and choose the parts of the Bible they want to obey. This person seems to think that the Word is like the buffet line at a local restaurant where you just pick the food you want and leave the rest.

There are some church goers who salivate over teachings on money and healing, but they tune out when the pastor teaches on witnessing, helping and/or anything else that doesn't float their spiritual boat.

Third, there is the TEMPORARY DOER ...

The temporary doer does the Word for a season ... as long as things are going the way he or she wants.

A temporary doer will tithe until the bills from Christmas roll in or there is some other bump in their financial journey ... then the excuses start.

God doesn't like excuses for not being a doer of His Word. He loves us but will hold us accountable for what we do or don't do.

1 John 2:28 in the Message Bible says:

> "And now, children, stay with Christ. Live deeply in Christ. Then we'll be ready for him when he appears, ready to receive him with open arms, with no cause for red-faced guilt or lame excuses when he arrives."

Fourth, there is the CONVENIENT DOER ...

As the name implies, a convenient doer only does what and when things are convenient.

There are no asterisks in James 1:22 with notes of exclusion at the bottom of the page. The scripture doesn't tell us to be a doer of the Word only if it's convenient ... or when we feel like it. No, the Word says to be a **Doer of the Word** ... and that means 24/7.

A great scriptural example of this is found in Luke 14:16-20 in the New Living Translation which says:

> "Jesus replied with this story: 'A man prepared a great feast and sent out many invitations. When the banquet was ready, he sent his servant to tell the guests, "Come, the banquet is ready." But they all began making excuses. One said, "I have just bought a field and must inspect it. Please excuse me." Another said, "I have just bought five pairs of oxen, and I want to try them out. Please excuse me." Another said, "I now have a wife, so I can't come." ' "

In Verses 18, 19 and 20 we see three separate excuses why it was not convenient for the people to attend the party. One used a new purchase of property as an excuse. Another one used work (his new oxen) as an excuse. And in Verse 20, the last man used his wife as an excuse.

What if Jesus had been a convenient doer of the Word? Do you think He would have ever died on the cross for you and me? I doubt it.

How would you feel if your employer were to tell

you that it's not convenient for them to give you a paycheck?

I think you get the picture.

Fifth, there is the COMMITTED DOER …

This is the person who is committed to doing whatever he or she is asked to do.

If they agree to volunteer for a function at church ... they're always there and on time.

If a person is committed to tithing, they will do so regardless of their temporary economic circumstances.

If a person is committed, they will be faithful to their God regardless of how great the temptation may be to sleep in or skip out.

If a person is a committed doer ... they will always be doing what pleases God in their personal life and commitments.

Sixth, there is the EFFECTIVE DOER …

It's one thing to do something ... to be committed ... but it's an entirely different matter to do it effectively.

James 1:25 in the New American Standard Bible says:

> "But one who looks intently at the perfect law,

the law of liberty, and abides by it, not having become a forgetful hearer but an effectual doer, this man will be blessed in what he does."

The New Living Translation says:

"But if you look carefully into the perfect law that sets you free, and if you do what it says and don't forget what you heard, then God will bless you for doing it."

I've know people who've made a commitment ... even honored that commitment, but they weren't effective in what they were doing.

Our ultimate goal in life as an effective doer of the Word is to be profitable to God and the establishment of His kingdom.

2 Timothy 4:11 says:

"Only Luke is with me. Take Mark, and bring him with thee: for he is profitable to me for the ministry."

We should be such a committed and effective doer of the Word that what we do will be deemed by God as profitable to Him and the Kingdom.

Finally I would like to share Luke 6:46 with you:

"And why call ye me, Lord, Lord, and do not

the things which I say?"

Seven words ... for your success.

READ YOUR BIBLE ... DO WHAT IT SAYS.

5 Hindrances to Your Surplus

I asked my friend Doug one day ... how he was doing, and I'll always remember his answer. He said, "Harold, for several years I'm been maintaining, and now I'm ready to move into surplus."

Surplus ... that word ignited in my spirit ... so I looked surplus up in the Merriam-Webster Collegiate Dictionary where it is defined as:

> **"the amount that remains when use or need is satisfied."**

I like that ... the amount that remains ... that's surplus.

It reminded me of Proverbs 3:10 in the Amplified Bible which describes what happens when you honor the Lord with your firstfruits:

> *"So shall your storage places be filled with plenty ..."*

Storage places are used for surplus.

I've obviously heard the word "surplus" before ... even preached about it in the context of the widow in Luke 21:4. The Amplified Bible says:

> "For they all gave out of their abundance (their **surplus**); but she has contributed out of her lack and her want, putting in all that she had on which to live."

Even though the story of the widow and her last two mites is familiar ... it's well worth reviewing again.

Mark 12:41-42 says:

> "And Jesus sat over against the treasury, and beheld how the people cast money into the treasury: and many that were rich cast in much. And there came a certain poor widow, and she threw in two mites, which make a farthing."

Jesus pulled a chair over where He could get a good view of how much people gave.

Can you imagine what would happen on Sunday morning if your pastor walked among the pews observing what everyone put into the offering?

Some "saint" would be complaining on the evening news about how "all the man of God is interested in ... is money." Such foolishness ... sadly ... does go on.

God does not tell you to give based on what's in your wallet, pocketbook or checking account.

Mark 12:43 says:

> "And he called unto him his disciples, and saith unto them, Verily I say unto you, That this poor widow hath cast more in, than all they which have cast into the treasury."

This poor widow did not give what was convenient or typical ... the scripture says that she cast in all ... everything she had ... not just her surplus ... but **all her living.**

Luke 21:4 in the Amplified Bible says:

> "For they all gave out of their abundance (their surplus); but she has contributed out of her lack and her want, putting in **all that she had on which to live.**"

The precious seed the widow sowed moved Jesus so much that she was memorialized in scripture.

Surplus is also used where Joseph advises Pharaoh how to handle the upcoming famine.

Genesis 41:48 in the Amplified Bible says:

> "And he gathered up all the [**surplus**] food of the seven [good] years in the land of Egypt

and stored up the food in the cities; he stored away in each city the food from the fields around it."

There is a key thought in this passage ... you don't use, spend or deplete all that you have during the good years.

<u>When the American economy was booming ... people were buying, spending and charging as if there was no tomorrow</u>. If it looked good, sounded good, felt good ... they bought it.

I'm not cursing the past or condemning those who made unwise spending decisions, as I have done that, too. However, I'm saying that not having a saving plan is foolish ... and opens us to the consequences of shortage ... famine or economic hard times.

Proverbs 21:20 in The Living Bible says:

"The wise man saves for the future, but the foolish man spends whatever he gets."

Your savings should be designed to give you choices about how you live in your future ... allowing you to improve the quality of your life.

However, if you spend everything you get ... then when there's an economic downturn, you're at someone else's mercy. Your assets will be exposed and the quality of your life threatened by shortage.

"Surplus is Good."

I was familiar with both the use of the word "surplus" in the scriptures dealing with the widow and her two mites as well as the story of Joseph creating a surplus of grain during the seven years of plenty.

But I felt there was something else the Lord wanted me to see. Why else would the word "surplus" have so ignited my spirit?

As I sought the Lord and started scanning scriptures I came across Deuteronomy 28:11 in the Amplified Bible:

> "And the Lord shall make you have a **surplus** of prosperity, through the fruit of your body, of your livestock, and of your ground, in the land which the Lord swore to your fathers to give you."

The first thing that stirred in me ... was ***"the Lord shall make you have a surplus of prosperity."***

Your surplus of prosperity is not based on you ... although <u>your obedience to God's Word will determine whether or not you receive what God has in store for you</u>.

Our actions and reactions will either positively or negatively determine our destiny.

Note that we will not just be prosperous, but we will have a surplus of prosperity.

Luke 12:32 says:

> "Fear not, little flock; for it is your Father's good pleasure to give you the kingdom."

Here's a question ... if it's God's will to give us the kingdom, then why are so many people struggling? Here are five hindrances to your surplus of prosperity:

Fear ... of the unknown. Fear of failure.

Doubt ... that God will do what He says He will do in His Word.

Anxiety ... over the current economic and political landscape.

Hesitation ... to give what God says to give because of our perceived limitations and lack.

Disbelief ... over whether everything promised in the Bible applies to "me."

The great news is that once you recognize that fear, doubt, anxiety, hesitation and/or disbelief is holding you back from receiving your surplus of prosperity ... you can deal with them and eliminate those five hindrances out of your life.

Child of God, the Word is clear ... it's your Heavenly Father's pleasure to give you the kingdom ... a surplus of prosperity.

God wants us living in abundance ... in surplus. Our Heavenly Father wants to give us *"... a rich and satisfying life"* as described in John 10:10 in the New Living Translation.

In fact, **the words "surplus" and "abundance" are used interchangeably in the story of the widow with the two mites.**

Luke 21:4 in the Amplified Bible gives a very clear illustration of this.

> *"For they all gave out of their **abundance** (their **surplus**); but she has contributed out of her lack and her want, putting in all that she had on which to live."*

Make no mistake about it ... God wants you to have a surplus ... for Him it's a matter of keeping His Word. Let's look at Deuteronomy 28:11 in the Amplified Bible one more time:

> *"And the Lord shall make you have a **surplus** of prosperity, through the fruit of your body, of your livestock, and of your ground, in the land which the Lord swore to your fathers to give you."*

God has no choice in the matter if you want to look at it that way ... **as long as you're obedient and faithful to His Word, then He must give you** *"...a* *surplus of prosperity"* **because He swore to your fathers that He would.**

Remember, God is not a man that He should lie (Numbers 23:19). **God must keep His Word ... which means that He not only must but will give you a "surplus of prosperity."**

Avoiding Spiritual Icebergs

The year 2012 was the 100th anniversary of the sinking of the RMS Titanic.

There have been numerous movies made about the sinking of the "unsinkable" Titanic. It's generally known that the ship was 882 feet long, 92 feet wide and the height of its eight decks was about 11 stories.

It's also well known that the Titanic hit a massive iceberg just before midnight on April 14, 1912 and less than four hours later sank to a watery grave in the icy waters of the North Atlantic along with 1,157 people.

The most expensive one-way first class ticket on the Titanic was $4,350 which would be roughly $101,000 in today's currency. The cheapest one-way ticket at the time was $35 which would be $812.58 in today's money. Just as a frame of reference, the average working person at the time made $6 a week, which meant it would take about 6 weeks' pay to buy the cheapest ticket.

There are so many fascinating stories about the

Titanic, but I'm only going to tell you one more lest I stray from what I feel led to share today.

There were two other ships involved in the Titanic tragedy ... the Californian and the Carpathia.

The captain of the Californian was a cautious man ... not willing to take chances and hesitant to get involved ... much like some church-going Christians today. He slept during the night and only sailed to assist at first light.

The other ship was the Carpathia. Arthur H. Rostron was its captain. **He was known to be a man of action and prayer.** When he learned of the plight of the Titanic he immediately ordered his ship on a rescue mission even in the face of great danger.

Captain Rostron issued orders preparing his passengers and crew members to assist in the rescue. As a traveling precaution in the frigid waters ... he added six men to key lookout positions, even including himself in that onerous duty. It's reported that the captain was on the wing of the ship's bridge, and that he prayed along the way.

The Carpathia arrived at the Titanic's last reported location at 4 AM and began rescuing survivors from the lifeboats. As the sun rose on the morning of April 15th ... it revealed the Carpathia surrounded by icebergs, many of which weren't seen by the extra lookouts positioned in key places by Captain Rostron.

The reason the Carpathia survived its rescue mission is simple ... it was prayer. James Bisset, the second officer of the Carpathia, reported that Captain Rostron prayed the entire time.

The way for each of us to avoid spiritual icebergs is to pray.

Now back to what I feel stirred to share with you today.

The people who bought the tickets for the maiden voyage of the Titanic were guaranteed passage for a price, yet the vast majority never completed their journey.

A guarantee is only as good as the company or the person backing up the guarantee. There are people who make guarantees but have neither the intention nor the ability to back up what they've promised.

Aren't you glad that we serve a God who ALWAYS backs up His guarantees?

2 Samuel 23:5 in the New Living Translation says:

> "Is it not my family God has chosen? Yes, he has made an everlasting covenant with me. His agreement is arranged and **guaranteed** in every detail. He will ensure my safety and success."

The Titanic guaranteed the safety of its passengers, but there were only enough lifeboats for roughly one-third of the people. In addition, the crew never had a lifeboat drill.

As a Child of God, we have an everlasting covenant, and EVERY detail is GUARANTEED. The Creator of Heaven and Earth, our Provider, will ensure our success.

The activation of our guarantee is based entirely on each of us. **When we follow His Word ... obey His direction ... then our everlasting covenant is guaranteed in every detail.**

Romans 4:16 in the Amplified Bible says:

> "Therefore, [inheriting] the promise is the outcome of faith and depends [entirely] on faith, in order that it might be given as an act of grace (unmerited favor), to make it stable and valid and **guaranteed** to all his descendants—not only to the devotees and adherents of the Law, but also to those who share the faith of Abraham, who is [thus] the father of us all."

The successful implementation of our covenant is based entirely on our faith. We are given the directions and roadmap to success ... our guarantee is backed by His Word but activated by our faithfulness.

There will be times when we place impediments on our journey to the debt-free lifestyle.

We will encounter dangerous spiritual and financial icebergs that stand in our way ... some will be visible ... others will be submerged and hidden from view ... but prayer and obedience to His Word will steer us safely toward our destination ... which is the covenant manifestation in our lives.

The challenges we face ... financial or otherwise ... may be treacherous but we need to praise God in every situation ... because He has created the ultimate GUARANTEED return on everything our hands find to do that bring glory and honor to Him.

So, let's praise Him for what He's done, is doing and will continue to do in our lives as we prove ourselves faithful.

I feel led to share portions of Psalm 111:1-10 in the Message Bible which say:

> *"Hallelujah! I give thanks to God with everything I've got ... God's works are so great, worth a lifetime of study—endless enjoyment! Splendor and beauty mark his craft; His generosity never gives out. His miracles are his memorial— This God of Grace, this God of Love ... proved to his people that he could do what he said...He ordered his Covenant kept forever. He's so personal and holy, worthy of our respect. The good life begins in the fear of God— Do that and you'll know the blessing of God. His Hallelujah lasts forever!"*

When we follow His Word ... we are faithful to His direction ... then He guarantees every detail to ensure our ... safety and success.

When God directs our path we're more than survivors picked up on the lifeboats of life ... we are more than conquerors ... it's a GUARANTEED trip.

Here's the question of the day:

Are we more like the captain of the Californian ... cautious ... unconcerned about the potential loss of life of other people ... unwilling to take a step of faith ... unless we can clearly see where we're going?

Has anyone ever made a promise to you, then broken it? How did it make you feel? Have you ever broken a promise to someone else? How did you feel afterwards?

The Good News ... the Great News is ... there is someone who will NEVER break a promise to you.

Ephesians 1:14 in the New Living Translation says:

> *"The Spirit is God's guarantee that he will give us the inheritance he promised and that he has purchased us to be his own people. He did this so we would praise and glorify him."*

Put your name in this:

      God will give [Name] what He promised.

God is not a man, that he should lie, nor the son of man that he should repent.

I believe you are like the captain of the Carpathia ... people of action and prayer. There is one action I would encourage you to take today ... immediately, if possible.

I encourage you to recall an instance where God came through for you when you needed him. Write it down. It may be more than one instance. Regardless ... write it down.

If you didn't praise Him for His faithfulness at the time ... then you can do it now ... that's the best way I know to avoid spiritual icebergs.

As I close this teaching today ... I'm led to read Romans 4:20-21 which says:

> "He staggered not at the promise of God through unbelief; but was strong in faith, giving glory to God;
>
> "And being fully persuaded that, what he had promised, he was able also to perform."

God told me ... that you have the faith of Abraham ... use it ... to experience His unfulfilled promises BEING fulfilled.

Last night, Asako posted this praise comment on my Facebook page:

"Yesterday I sowed a seed on line to TLC (Triumphant Life Church). Three potential customers called me today. Glory to God. I have no doubts. The Lord will give me all three."

If you would like more insightful information on the three leadership styles of the captains of the Titanic, Californian and the Carpathia ... I highly recommend you read *Leadership, Management and The Five Essentials for Success* by Rick Joyner.

6 Things to Know If You Want God to Be Good to You

Day 11

If someone stole your wages ... how **would you respond?**

If someone withheld what was rightfully yours ... **what would you say?**

If someone lied to you time after time ... **what would you think?**

If someone tricked you in a way that would affect your family for years to come ... **how would you react?**

If someone close to you continually tried to deceive you ... **what would you do?**

Your reaction to adversity ... to wrongdoing ... to treachery ... will determine your destiny.

That reaction will **either propel you to success** or **destine you to failure.**

It will determine whether or not God is good to you or is able to help you.

Consider the case of Jacob.

If you think you have a **bad ... arrogant ... deceitful ... crooked boss** ... one who **withholds your wages** or **treats you unfairly**, then you haven't met Laban, Jacob's boss and father-in-law.

Jacob worked seven years to marry Laban's beautiful younger daughter, only to have Laban secretly switch daughters on their wedding night and trick Jacob into a marriage with his "plain" older daughter.

Laban was crooked, crooked, crooked, and a real tightwad! **Ten times, Laban changed Jacob's compensation program!**

Even in the midst of a conniving work environment ... Jacob never wavered. He always did the right and honorable thing even if his boss and relative didn't. Jacob stayed strong in his faith and obedient to God.

As a **result of his faithfulness in seemingly unbearable circumstances**, God honored Jacob with His favor and wealth.

After many years of working faithfully for Laban, God instructed Jacob to "return to the land of thy fathers." Jacob was willing to obey. But before he left, Jacob revealed to Laban's daughters the amazing divine principle of taking the wealth of the wicked and **giving it to the just**, the principle that had been operating in his life as he worked for their father, Laban.

I suggest you write these verses down and review them very carefully, for they **provide a major breakthrough in understanding the mind of God.** Let them destroy any previous conceptions you may have had about what God will do for His children if we do things His way.

Genesis 31:6-9 says:

> *"And ye know that with all my power I have served your father. And your father hath deceived me, and changed my wages ten times; but God suffered him not to hurt me. If he said thus, the speckled shall be thy wages, then all the cattle bare speckled: and if he said thus, the ringstraked shall be thy hire; then bare all the cattle ringstraked. Thus* **God hath taken away the cattle of your father, and given them to me."**

God took the wealth of Laban, a wicked man who kept changing the rules of Jacob's compensation program, and gave his wealth to Jacob.

Laban could do nothing to stop the transfer of his wealth to Jacob, once God started the process. The process started because Jacob turned to God for justice and guidance in his adversity.

When Laban said he **would pay Jacob in only the speckled cattle** that came forth from the herd, God made all the cattle have speckled young.

When Laban said he **would only pay in striped cattle**, then **God made all the calves striped.**

Jacob endured hardship ... but **God protected him**. He endured lies and deception for over 20 years ... but <u>see this very clearly</u>: **he later told his brother Esau that God had been good to him.**

Genesis 33:10 in the Message Bible says:

> "Jacob said, 'Please. If you can find it in your heart to welcome me, accept these gifts. When I saw your face, it was as the face of God smiling on me. Accept the gifts I have brought for you. **God has been good to me and I have more than enough.**' Jacob urged the gifts on him and Esau accepted."

Jacob made an important decision in the midst of his adversity. He <u>chose not to **let** his circumstances make him bitter</u>. He **committed his future and fortune to God** which allowed Jacob to later look back and declare his life was good ... all because he **chose to follow the Lord in the midst of adverse circumstances**. <u>How many good-hearted but ill-treated people miss this</u>?

<u>God took the wealth of the **wicked** Laban and gave it to the **just** Jacob</u>. And the God Jacob served yesterday is the very same God you serve today and **your children will serve tomorrow.**

It's important for us to understand ... that **regardless**

of the unfairness, <u>dishonesty and treachery we've had to live</u> with or <u>travel through</u> ... we are the ones who choose what our outcome will be.

There are **six things to know if you want God to be good to you.**

First, do everything you do as unto the Lord even in a hostile environment.

Colossians 3:23 in the Amplified Bible says:

> *"Whatever may be your task, work at it heartily (from the soul), as [something done] for the Lord and not for men."*

Now listen to the Message Bible translation of Colossians 3:23 which says:

> *"Do your best. Work from the heart for your real Master, for God, confident that you'll get paid in full when you come into your inheritance. Keep in mind always that the ultimate Master you're serving is Christ."*

Second, God will never leave nor forsake you.

Romans 8:31 in the Amplified Bible says:

> *"What then shall we say to [all] this? If God is for us, who [can be] against us? [Who can be our foe, if God is on our side?]"*

Hebrews 13:8 says:

> "Jesus Christ the same yesterday, and today, and forever."

Third, your enemies will become God's enemies.

Deuteronomy 20:4 says:

> "For the LORD your God is he that goeth with you, to fight for you against your enemies, to save you."

Deuteronomy 20:4 in the Message Bible says:

> "In a few minutes you're going to do battle with your enemies. Don't waver in resolve. Don't fear. Don't hesitate. Don't panic. God, your God, is right there with you, fighting with you against your enemies, fighting to win."

Psalm 91:7 says:

> "A thousand shall fall at thy side, and ten thousand at thy right hand; but it shall not come nigh thee."

Psalm 136:24 in the Amplified Bible says:

> "And rescued us from our enemies, for His mercy and loving-kindness endure forever."

Fourth, everything the enemy has stolen from you will be repaid sevenfold.

Proverbs 6:31 says:

> "But if he be found, he shall restore sevenfold; he shall give all the substance of his house."

Joel 2:25 in the Message Bible says:

> "I'll make up for the years of the locust …"

Fifth, you are more than a conqueror.

Romans 8:37 in the Amplified Bible says:

> "Yet amid all these things we are more than conquerors and gain a surpassing victory through Him Who loved us."

Sixth, always sing praises to God because He is good to you.

Psalm 13:6 in the New Living Translation says:

> "I will sing to the Lord because he is good to me."

Child of God, I want you to be able to say like Jacob …

"God has been good to me and I have more than enough."

<u>You may feel like you've been living in the valley of the shadow of death</u>, but fear no evil because God is more powerful ... omnipotent ... omnipresent ... loving ... just ... <u>forgiving and generous</u> ... <u>than anybody else in the valley</u> ... and <u>He's right there with you</u>.

When you do what's right in His sight ... **regardless of what's happening around you**, then you will be able to say as Jacob said:

"God has been good to me and I have more than enough."

7 Reasons Why You Give To Get

Day 12

Dr. Martin Luther King, Jr. said:

"Nothing in the world is more dangerous than sincere ignorance and conscientious stupidity."

As I reflected on this quote I was reminded of a conversation I had with someone in a position of authority ... I'd like to call him "Goofy," but that would be disrespectful, so I won't.

This person was telling me that we should never **Give** to **Get.**

Truthfully, I couldn't believe how a person of this man's standing could demonstrate such ignorance of the Word.

The good thing about being ignorant [not knowing the truth] is that there's hope for you. Ignorance is not an incurable disease.

It can be overcome with the Word by those who are willing to know the truth.

Here are seven reasons why you Give to Get.

1. If you <u>give your heart to Jesus, then you get abundant and eternal life</u>.

Romans 10:9 says:

> "That if thou shalt confess with thy mouth the Lord Jesus, and shalt believe in thine heart that God hath raised him from the dead, thou shalt be saved."

John 10:10 says:

> "... I am come that they might have life, and that they might have it more abundantly."

God gave His only begotten Son Jesus ... so He could reap a harvest of souls.

Titus 2:14 in the Amplified Bible says:

> "Who gave Himself on our behalf that He might redeem us (purchase our freedom) from all iniquity and purify for Himself a people [to be peculiarly His own, people who are] eager and enthusiastic about [living a life that is good and filled with] beneficial deeds."

We give to get ... salvation and a life that is good and filled with beneficial deeds.

2. **If you want to have a closer relationship with the Lord and sweet communion with the Holy Spirit, then you <u>give your time to get into His presence</u>.**

2 Timothy 2:15 in the Amplified Bible says:

"Study and be eager and do your utmost to present yourself to God approved (tested by trial), a workman who has no cause to be ashamed, correctly analyzing and accurately dividing [rightly handling and skillfully teaching] the Word of Truth."

There are way too many believers who want the benefits and blessings of God without the relationship. The only way you have relationship is to spend time in His presence.

I love my fine wife, Bev, but if I only spend two hours with her on Sunday morning and an hour with her on Wednesday night, we're not going to have much of a relationship. If you want to have an intimate relationship with your Heavenly Father, then you need to spend time in His Presence ... and in His Word.

Yes, you give your time to get into His presence.

3. **You have to <u>give your whole heart if you want to get ... and experience ... a happy marriage</u>.**

Without commitment, the vows you take at the altar may only last as long as the honeymoon. It takes more for a happy marriage than picking the right china patterns or an active sex life. Just telling it straight here.

You've got to invest time in each other. Learn to forgive when it's not your fault and remember that having the last word doesn't mean that you're right or you won the argument.

Total commitment says: I will love you and **I'm willing to ride the waves of life even in a hurricane so that our marriage doesn't wipe out.**

Commitment brings rewards.

4. You have to give up what's unhealthy if you want to get a healthier life.

Really it's easy…if you live and eat right and throw in some exercise, you can have a long life that will satisfy you, according to Psalm 91:16.

Your exercise program must consist of more than walking to the food pantry and grabbing a Twinkie between commercials. Is exercise easy and discipline free? Don't you be goofy; it takes commitment, but it's worth it.

You didn't get overweight overnight, and you're not going to change immediately … but change you must.

5. You have to give time to your children to get a legacy.

In Proverbs 13:22 the New King James Version says:

"A good man leaves an inheritance to his children's children ..."

This inheritance doesn't just refer to material wealth but also the inheritance of all of God's blessings and character that we desire for our children. How will they **get** that impartation unless you **give** them your time?

When was the last time that you spent ten minutes with your children and/or grandchildren just talking with them about what's important in their lives?

If they know how interested you are in their lives ... even when it's not convenient ... they'll be more inclined to listen to what you have to say.

6. You have to give time to preparation before you'll ever get promotion.

It would be goofy for you to go to your boss and say, "If you give me a raise, you'll get a better job performance from me." It doesn't work that way.

You want a promotion, a raise in pay or a better job? Go to work early, stay late. Forty hours is for people who just want to get by.

If you want to get ahead, turn the television off and prepare your mind. Read books, listen to CDs and prepare yourself mentally for the promotion awaiting you.

Don't think you have time? If you spend 30 minutes a day (Monday through Friday) watching television ... that amounts to 130 hours a year, or over 16 work days. That's the same amount of time most people get for their annual vacation

Everyone in the world has the same amount of time. It's how you choose to use it that separates the men from the boys ... the women from the girls.

Would your career and income possibilities be different if you invested that time in, say, your mind?

If you give learning the time, you'll get the promotion.

7. You have to <u>give money before you'll ever get a financial harvest</u>.

Why does the Bible say that we should give?

First, it is an act of worship; a reasonable response to all God has done for us (Romans 12:1; 2 Corinthians 8:8-9).

Second, our giving must reflect more than just lip service (Matthew 25:31-46). For where your treasure is, there your heart will be also (Matthew 6:21).

Third, we should give because the Lord Jesus (Luke 12:33) **and his apostles** (2 Corinthians 8:7) **taught us to give.**

Fourth, in the scriptures God promises rewards for giving (Luke 12:33).

I have a financial planner who always gives me great advice. He has never given me a bad tip. The return on the investments He recommends brings a far greater return than the Wall Street average.

Bottom line, if you sow ... you reap. Hear me clearly, Child of God, tough times are not the time to stop giving. It is a time to give with confidence knowing that God will bring the blessing.

2 Corinthians 9:6-7 in the New American Standard Bible tells us:

> *"Now this I say, he who sows sparingly will also reap sparingly, and he who sows bountifully will also reap bountifully. Each one must do just as he has purposed in his heart, not grudgingly or under compulsion, for God loves a cheerful giver."*

By this time you should realize that Goofy was just being what his name implied. He was trying to sound "holy" when talking about seedtime and harvest.

Understand this: The new trend of being "politically correct" is only good if it is scripturally correct.

How You Can Lack Nothing

I thank the Lord for His peace, protection, promotion, provision, power and the possibilities for today! And yes, I was praying for you as well.

I was led to 1 Thessalonians 4:11-12 in the King James Version of the Bible:

> *"And that ye study to be quiet, and to do your own business, and to work with your own hands, as we commanded you;* that ye may walk honestly toward them that are without, and that **ye may have lack of nothing**.*"*

First, I was taken by the phrase *"study to be quiet."* So I asked the Lord how you would "study to be quiet." I looked up "study" in The ESV English-Greek Reverse Interlinear New Testament ... and it's more properly translated as *aspire to a goal*.

That's why **the Amplified Bible translation of 1 Thessalonians 4:11 says:**

> *"... make it your ambition and definitely endeavor to be quiet."*

In essence, our goal ... our ambition should be to live a "quiet life." Now, lest you think that the Word is telling us to become monks ... consider that the word "quiet" also means *rest*.

One of our primary goals or ambitions should be to rest before Him. (I'm smiling as I write this.)

During the time I spent as Pastor of Administration at First Assembly of God Church in Goldsboro, North Carolina, I started a program called "Network Six."

Every day of the week except Sunday, the men of the church would gather at 6 AM for a 15-minute teaching ... then we would have corporate and individual prayer until 7 AM.

Each month, I would pick a topic and have a different man share his revelation on the subject for 15 minutes or less. Afterwards, we'd have a corporate prayer for 15 minutes ... then the men would spread throughout the church and pray ... individually.

I most often prayed prostrate on the floor. I will always remember the morning when I was awakened (yes, I confess, I fell asleep) by one of the men who told me it was 7 AM. Trying to make light of the situation, I smiled and told him that I was "resting before the Lord."

He smiled and said, "It's good you were resting, but I

don't think the Lord was able to because of the way you were snoring."

Needless to say, today, I'm talking about a different kind of "resting in Him."

It should be our ambition to lead a restful, quiet life where we're able to focus on Him and define our lives in relation to Him. It's a matter of what we have made our personal priorities.

One of the things that I have to fight for ... in fact, it is one of the things that I jealously guard ... is my time with the Lord.

There are mornings where I feel the press of impending tasks that need to be completed. **The enemy would like for me to delay my Daily Bible Reading and time with the Lord ... because he knows that meditation time deferred is rarely, if ever, made up.**

Truthfully, 1 Thessalonians 4:11 contains real insight as to how every believer should live his or her life.

> *"And that ye study to be quiet, and to do your own business, and to work with your own hands, as we commanded you."*

This verse is saying that during our rest, our quiet time, **we should only be concerned with doing the things that God has commanded us to do.**

Here are five things that 1 Thessalonians 4:11 is telling us to do:

1. **Study ... make it your personal ambition.**

2. **Be quiet ... restful ... free from outside distractions.**

3. **Mind your own business ... be accountable for your own life.**

4. **Work with your hands ... be productive.** (Back in the day, it was an agrarian society and people worked with their hands more than their heads.)

5. **Follow God's instructions.**

Let's look at 1 Thessalonians 4:12 which says:

"That ye may walk honestly toward them that are without, and that ye may have lack of nothing."

Personalize this verse.

"That [Name] may walk honestly toward them that are without, and [Name] may have lack of nothing."

Whatever your name is ... Diane & Dave ... Randy & Laurel ... Al & Jenine ... make it yours.

First, we're told to walk honestly ... to be truthful ... to never lie. <u>If the verse is telling us to "walk honestly," that means that our natural tendency is to do just the opposite.</u>

When the scripture says "walk," it's demonstrating movement through the course of the day. Being honest is an absolute necessity whether it's at home, a PTA meeting or on the job.

Second, the scripture says that we're to be honest "toward them that are without." We need to carefully consider our actions ... as we're interacting on a daily basis with a lot of folks who don't know Jesus. We may be one of their few examples.

For instance, don't borrow five bucks from an unbelieving coworker and forget to pay it back. I even heard of one goofy guy whose logic in not repaying a loan was that it was the wealth of the wicked laid up for the righteous. Surely, he'd never even read the Bible.

I'll tell you that when you borrow and don't repay ... you're anything but righteous.

How do your actions and reactions witness to your unbelieving coworkers?

The Living Bible translation of 1 Thessalonians 4:12 says:

> *"As a result, people who are not Christians will trust and respect you ..."*

God is showing us that our honesty toward others is one of the most important witnessing tools at our disposal. The Word says that even people who aren't Christians *"will trust and respect you."*

The best way to witness to your friends is not with a gospel tract but through the fruit of the spirit they see manifesting in your life day in and day out.

When we spend time with Him ... when we treat others right ... when we acknowledge His role in our daily lives ... then we can experience the blessing found in the last part of 1 Thessalonians 4:12 which in The Living Bible says:

> *"As a result, people who are not Christians will trust and respect you, and* **you will not need to depend on others for enough money to pay your bills."**

Right behavior yields the right results.

We will never have to depend on others for help whether through governmental assistance ... family or business loans ... or anything or anybody else. For those of you going through difficult times ... take comfort in this scripture.

Child of God, are you getting hold of this scripture?

Write it out on a 3X5 card and get it down in your spirit ... **"YOU WILL NEVER HAVE TO DEPEND ON**

OTHERS FOR ENOUGH MONEY TO PAY YOUR BILLS."

Personalize this quote for yourself:

"[Name] will never have to depend on others for enough money to pay [his/her] bills."

That's for you ... Mary ... Faith ... Nicole ...

Can somebody say Hallelujah!!

The Amplified Bible translation of 1 Thessalonians 4:12 says:

"So that you may bear yourselves becomingly and be correct and honorable and command the respect of the outside world, being dependent on nobody [self-supporting] and having need of nothing."

I find it significant that this translation says that we will "command the respect of the outside world" by being financially independent.

There will be no need for a special gift from a family member to help you make it through another month.

You will command the respect of non-believers because you're working and have no unmet needs.

In other words, our witness to non-believers is based on our ability to be financially free and independent.

Conversely, you can't be an effective witness if you're broke and always depending on somebody else to be your miracle manifestation ... to bail you out of every impending financial catastrophe.

That's not the way God wants you to live.

If you want to lack nothing in your life ... then study and meditate on 1 Thessalonians 4:11-12 ... your life will be enriched.

Answering the Right Question Meets Every Need

One of my favorite teachings is entitled, "Don't Be Hypnotized by the Appearance of Lack."

Matthew 14:15 in the New Living Translation says:

> *"That evening the disciples came to him and said, 'This is a remote place, and it's already getting late. Send the crowds away so they can go to the villages and buy food for themselves.'"*

The disciples brought Jesus a negative report.

Now get a picture of this ... those closest to Jesus ... those who had seen Him heal blinded eyes, restore lame limbs, and work mighty miracles ... those closest to Him were hypnotized by the appearance of lack.

The message was clear ... the disciples were saying, this is a "desert place" meaning there's nothing here ... no Chick-fil-A ... no Subway ... no Chinese buffet ... we'd better send the people home because there's nothing out here to eat.

Those closest to Jesus were still surveying situations with their natural eyes. They were bound by their circumstances. **Sometimes in life, we get so blinded by our situation that we can't focus on what possibilities are in front of us.**

In our own lives all too often those closest to us are the ones who bring the negative report, because they're also hypnotized by appearance of lack.

I always get fired up about this teaching ... however, today the Lord led me to read this account in the gospel of John. Let's look at John 6:5-13 in the New International Version:

> *"When Jesus looked up and saw a great crowd coming toward him, he said to Philip, 'Where shall we buy bread for these people to eat?' He asked this only to test him, for he already had in mind what he was going to do.*
>
> *"Philip answered him, 'Eight months' wages would not buy enough bread for each one to have a bite!'*
>
> *"Another of his disciples, Andrew, Simon Peter's brother, spoke up, 'Here is a boy with five small barley loaves and two small fish, but how far will they go among so many?'*
>
> *"Jesus said, 'Have the people sit down.' There*

was plenty of grass in that place, and the men sat down, about five thousand of them. Jesus then took the loaves, gave thanks, and distributed to those who were seated as much as they wanted. He did the same with the fish.

"When they had all had enough to eat, he said to his disciples, 'Gather the pieces that are left over. Let nothing be wasted.' So they gathered them and filled twelve baskets with the pieces of the five barley loaves left over by those who had eaten."

Now let's look at John 6:5 in the New International Version again. It says:

"When Jesus looked up and saw a great crowd coming toward him, he said to Philip, 'Where shall we buy bread for these people to eat?'"

The scriptures say that Jesus was testing Philip. John 6:6 in the New International Version says:

"He asked this only to test him, for he already had in mind what he was going to do."

Without question, Philip missed it. Jesus asked Philip "where" they could buy bread to eat, and Philip responded by totally ignoring the question that Jesus asked him.

Jesus wanted to know "where" and Philip was trying to figure out "how."

John 6:7 in the New International Version says:

> "Philip answered him, 'Eight months' wages would not buy enough bread for each one to have a bite!' "

According to the Holman Christian Standard Bible ... Philip said they only had about 200 denarii ... which according to the Amplified Bible was about $40. Regardless of the amount, Philip was ignoring the question that Jesus posed ... "where" they should buy the bread.

Philip was responding to what he perceived to be a financial question when in fact it was a question of faith.

Lest we too quickly condemn Philip ... **we need to ask ourselves how many times we have allowed fear and worry to grip our financial situations instead of claiming and confessing the precious promises of God.**

Andrew was more helpful than Philip, although it seems he still didn't see the complete potential for miracle manifestation.

John 6:8 in the Holman Christian Standard Bible says:

> "There is a lad here, which hath five barley loaves, and two small fishes: but what are they among so many?"

Philip had asked "how," and now Andrew is asking "what."

Once again, the wrong question is being answered ... but at least Andrew brought the little boy with the five barley loaves and two fishes.

In heaven ... one of the people I want to talk with is the little boy with the loaves and fishes. **To Andrew ... what the little boy had in his hand wasn't enough ... but to the boy it was everything he had, and he was willing to share.**

Now I'm going to say this again ... because I really want us to get it down inside of us.

Andrew did a good thing ... although he thought what was in the boy's hand was not enough to be multiplied to meet the need. Yet to the boy, what he was willing to offer was everything he had ... and it was more than enough to meet everybody's need ... with plenty left over.

Some of you may feel that what's in your hand at the moment is not enough to meet your need ... but when you release it into God's hands, it becomes more than enough to meet your needs ... with plenty left over to share with others.

2 Corinthians 9:7-8 in the New Living Translation says:

> *"**You must each decide in your heart how much to give.** And don't give reluctantly or in*

response to pressure. 'For God loves a person who gives cheerfully.' And God will generously provide all you need. Then you will always have everything you need and plenty left over to share with others."

Here's a truth that every believer needs to grasp.

<u>What you have in your hands right now is enough to meet every need that you have ... when you give it to Jesus</u>.

<u>In your hand ... it's not enough ... but in His hand, it's more than enough</u>.

When you hold on too tightly to what you have ... you're operating in limitation ... but when you release it, God then begins to increase it.

Jesus started with what He had ... offered it to God ... and in simple faith expected the increase. **He didn't allow the limited resources given by the little lad to stop Him from taking action ... He acted in faith on what He had available to him at the moment.**

Too many times, I've heard Christians complaining about what they don't have instead of praising God for what they do have.

As you examine your current financial situation ... regardless of how much debt you have or the balance or lack thereof in your investment portfolio ... it's important that you answer the right question.

Don't concern yourself with how God is going to deliver you from your current financial situation or mess ... the question is *where*.

***Where* does God want you to sow?**

The problem with a lack of food in John 6 was solved not by complaining or questioning but by giving. The little boy gave all he had to the work of the ministry and people were fed.

Not only that, there were twelve baskets full remaining ... the little boy who gave all he had was able to return home with increase and a powerful testimony of how Jesus had used what was in his hand to bless so many others.

When we read the Word of God, we must focus on what the book is saying ... not in light of our circumstances ... but in light of our faith in the Word of God ... and His ability to multiply what we have to meet every need.

Here is a good testimonial from one of my friends out there:

Denise from Harrisburg posted this on my Facebook wall this morning:

"One of my blessings is *The Spiritual Entrepreneur Guidebook*. It's like having a personal trainer who anticipates every challenge, and helps you rise above - facilitating thought conditioning where there have been failings before, and as noted in the reading just this morning:

"A word of encouragement during failure is worth far more than an hour of praise after success."

Joshua's 10 Success Secrets

Success is an attitude. Success is a habit. Success is a lifestyle. Success is easily available to anyone who wants it ... believes they can have it ... works for it ... never gives up and always ... always trusts God ... no matter what.

Success happens inside you before it ever happens around you. **There is a defining moment when you decide to take control of your own life and embrace the success that God wants you to achieve.**

Joshua **spent 20 years preparing for his divine destiny** ... his success as a leader for the Children of Israel. In the life and book of Joshua there are 10 success secrets that are critical to our future.

1st Step—See your goal.

It's not enough for you to believe for your goal ... you've got to see it ... you've got to know that it can be a reality in your life.

God not only promised Joshua that he would win the battle, He also wanted him to see the victory before it actually happened.

I want you to get this down in your spirit ... it is critical to moving the hand of God in your every circumstance.

One of the keys to Joshua's victory was the fact that God said, *"SEE, I have given [YOU] Jericho."* (Joshua 6:2)

God used the same principle in allowing Joshua to see the victory at Ai.

Joshua 8:1 says:

> *"... arise, go up to Ai:* **see***, I have given into thy hand the king of Ai, and his people, and his city, and his land."*

You need to see yourself debt free ... before you ever will be.

You need to see yourself being promoted ... employed ... healthy ... financially independent ... before you ever will be.

2nd Step—Arise and do something.

In Joshua 1:2 when Jehovah said, *"Arise, go over the Jordan,"* Joshua was ready.

He went into the Hebrew camp in Joshua 1:11 and said,

> *"Prepare ... for within three days you are to*

pass over this Jordan, to go in and possess the land which Jehovah your God giveth you to possess."

The Jordan River symbolizes any obstacle that stands between you and your goal. Oftentimes that barrier appears more difficult to penetrate than it really is …

The Jordan River wasn't very big … especially by our standards … it was more like a large creek … the children of Israel had been in the desert so long that it looked like an extraordinary body of water.

To the children of Israel it seemed huge because … it was primarily a psychological barrier.

When God says "Arise," it means start moving towards your goal … the thing you desire … the thing you've been believing for.

You've got a part to play in your own success.

Joshua 1:16 says:

> *"All that thou has commanded us we will do, and whithersoever thou sendest us we will go."*

If you want to be successful, you've got to see yourself going, arise (get started) and start moving toward your victory.

Arise … do something … success is coming to your house.

3rd Step—Say "Yes" to possibilities and "No" to excuses.

Too many believers do just the opposite … saying "yes" to excuses and "no" to possibilities. That needs to stop today. Let's explore some of the excuses.

"I'm too young." Tell this to Debbie Fields, founder and owner of Mrs. Fields Cookies, who was in her twenties when she achieved success, or Steve Jobs, founder of Apple Computers, who made his first million when he was twenty-three, his first ten million at twenty-four and his first 100 million at twenty-five.

"I'm too old." Work does not kill. Idleness, on the other hand, is often deadly; people who take early retirement often die younger than those who keep working.

Gandhi was 78 when he led India to independence.

Mother Theresa was 69 when she won the Nobel Peace Prize.

George Burns was 79 when he won his Oscar.

Colonel Sanders was 65 when he started Kentucky Fried Chicken.

Caleb was 80 years old when he said, "Give me my mountain."

"I'm not educated." Neither was fashion designer

Donna Karan. Thomas Edison left school before the age of sixteen. Microsoft's Bill Gates is a college dropout.

"I'm afraid of failure." We're born with two fears: falling and loud noises. All other fears are acquired.

Often deeply embedded within us, fear results from past failures, from a lack of confidence bred unknowingly by our parents or relatives, and it's enforced by society's general negative, short-sighted thinking.

I could go on ... but here's the bottom line ...

Just say "No" to doubt, fear and defeat.

<u>Say "Yes" to the greater opportunity that lies before you from the greater One that is in you</u>.

4th Step—Cleanse yourself of all unrighteousness ... sanctify yourself.

The next step in Joshua's master plan for success was to cross the Jordan River. In preparation for this, Joshua told the people to "sanctify" themselves ... meaning to cleanse themselves inwardly and outwardly ... with the promise.

Joshua 3:5 in the American Standard Version says:

> "For tomorrow, Jehovah will do wonders among you."

Joshua told the priests to go into the river and "stand still" just inside the water's edge, bearing the ark of the covenant (Joshua 3:8) ... and when they did so, the waters parted and the people passed over into the Promised Land.

Before you can cross over ... you need to sanctify yourself ... cleansing yourself of any and all unrighteousness ... but the good news is that He is faithful to cleanse us and forgive us of any and all unrighteousness. (I John 1:9)

5th Step—Speak words of life, victory and power to your situation.

Review the divine promises that assure you that successful results are your heritage by studying some of these great passages of the Bible.

Joshua 3:9 in the American Standard Version says:

> "And Joshua said unto the children of Israel, Come hither and hear the words of Jehovah your God."

6th Step—Eliminate all fear of failure.

Joshua 8:1 says:

> "And the LORD said unto Joshua, Fear not, neither be thou dismayed: take all the people of war with thee, and arise, go up ..."

7th Step—Know that God is on your side.

When your heart is right … seeking Him and His righteousness … then God will fight your battles.

Exodus 23:22 says:

> "But if thou shalt indeed obey his voice, and do all that I speak; then I will be an enemy unto thine enemies, and an adversary unto thine adversaries."

8th Step—Realize the part you have to play in your own steps to success.

Joshua 1:8 says:

> "This book of the law shall not depart out of thy mouth; but thou shalt meditate therein day and night, that thou mayest observe to do according to all that is written therein: for then thou shalt make thy way prosperous, and then thou shalt have good success."

If you think you can, or if you think you can't—you're right.

9th Step—Keep focused on your success.

Either read the Bible or listen to CDs or MP3s of the Bible Daily … you will change in direct proportion to the Words you hear from Him.

Nobody else can do this for you. You must pursue the Word of God for yourself.

One of the best ways to stay focused is reading books and listening to teachings that will stir your faith and God-given creativity.

10th Step—Give thanks.

As the Hebrews passed through the Jordan River, Joshua instructed them to pick up twelve stones from the water—one for each tribe of Israel.

After arriving on the edge of the Promised Land, they build an altar at Gilgal using the twelve stones as a memorial of thanksgiving to Jehovah for having divinely delivered Israel's twelve tribes. (Joshua 4:19-24)

When you have passed through troubled waters and are on dry land again ... always give thanks ... Don't take the good you have for granted.

Get out in front of your battle and begin praising God for the things that He has already done in your life ... the things that He's doing at this very moment and the things that He's going to do.

Day 16

How to Get What You Ask For

Do you remember the title of your pastor's message from last Sunday?

What was the key point in his teaching?

Do you recall what I taught on our RichThoughts for Breakfast conference call three days ago or a week ago?

Do you remember the title of the lead article in last week's edition of the RichThoughts email I sent to you?

How many of the key points can you write down from the last CD you listened to?

I'm not trying to make you feel bad ... if you don't remember. Truthfully, that's the normal response.

It's a scientific fact that <u>**you will forget 50% of what you've read or heard within three hours of reading or hearing it.**</u> And sadly, twenty-four hours later you will have forgotten 50% of that information. By the end of 30 days, most people will recall less than 5% of that ... in other words only 2½ percent of the original material you were exposed to.

Brother Harold, are you telling me it's not worth my time to read or listen to new teaching material?

Not at all, but **I'm suggesting a different style of learning ... that will allow you to get whatever you ask for.**

2 Timothy 2:15 says:

> "**Study** to shew thyself approved unto God, a workman that needeth not to be ashamed, rightly dividing the word of truth."

The scripture says "study." It doesn't say "read once," "glance over" or "speed read through." The Word says "study," and I know the Holy Spirit used that Word for a reason.

Study is defined in dictionary.com as **"application of the mind to the acquisition of knowledge, as by reading, investigation, or reflection."**

As I read the definition of "study," it quickened in my spirit that the real process of "studying to show yourself approved" is contained in this definition.

Study is the acquisition of knowledge by reading, investigating and reflecting.

It's simple, really ... **studying is a seed that you plant and the harvest is knowledge that you acquire.**

In fact, the scripture says in Mark 4:24 in the Amplified Bible that you will receive back more than you sow.

> *"And He said to them, Be careful what you are hearing. The measure [of thought and study] you give [to the truth you hear] will be the measure [of virtue and knowledge] that comes back to you--**and more [besides] will be given to you who hear.**"*

Your study of the Word is best done in His presence.

1 Chronicles 16:8-12 in the Message Bible says:

> *"Thank God! Call out his Name! Tell the whole world who he is and what he's done! Sing to him! Play songs for him! Broadcast all his wonders! Revel in his holy Name, God-seekers, be jubilant! Study God and his strength, seek his presence day and night; **Remember all the wonders he performed, the miracles and judgments that came out of his mouth ...**"*

When you study the Word of God you receive an immediate benefit, but there is also a progressive benefit to your children.

1 Chronicles 28:8 in the Message Bible says:

> "And now, in this public place, all Israel looking on and God listening in, as God's people, obey and study every last one of the commandments of your God so that you can make the most of living in this good land and pass it on intact to your children, insuring a good future."

Studying the Word is the key to your success in life.

Joshua 1:8 in the New Living Translation says:

> "Study this Book of Instruction continually. Meditate on it day and night so you will be sure to obey everything written in it. Only then will you prosper and succeed in all you do."

Something else just stirred in me about this scripture … so let's look at 2 Timothy 2:15 one more time.

> "Study to shew thyself approved unto God, a workman that needeth not to be ashamed, rightly dividing the word of truth."

According to the Strong's Concordance the word "workman" is the Greek word ***ergates*** (G2040) and it means:

> "a workman, labourer."

However, it is from the root word *ergon* (G2041) and it means:

"**any product whatever, anything accomplished by hand, art, industry, or mind; an act, deed, thing done.**"

A "workman" is someone who gets things done in such a manner that there can be no criticism of his or her efforts or deeds.

In fact, their deeds will be of a worthwhile nature with no complaints from upper management. **(That's a cool way to refer to God, as upper management.)**

Through this revelation, I felt the Lord impressing me to share a new study technique for all of us.

First, read the book without distraction.

Second, read the book again and this time use a yellow highlighter to mark key phrases, sentences or thoughts that stir your faith.

Third, read the book with a notepad so you can write out the things that prompt a call to change in your life. I suggest using a computer if one is available as notes have a way of getting lost.

Finally, read the book again reviewing only the highlights and your notes.

When it comes to CDs, I recommend you listen to it twice before you begin to take notes. I also find that listening to CDs with earphones increases my comprehension of what's being said.

In taking notes, you will need the ability to stop the CD and write notes on what you've just heard. If you're driving while listening … pause the CD and speak your notes into your smartphone.

After taking notes, listen to the CD again and review your notes. You will be amazed at the number of nuggets you will add to what you've already written. I also recommend that these notes be entered in a Word document on your computer for easier access in the future.

There is a reason the scripture says that faith comes by hearing and hearing by the Word of God (Romans 10:17).

Years ago I remember hearing Dr. Fred Price say that faith comes by hearing and hearing and hearing and hearing and hearing and hearing the Word of God. There is much truth in that statement.

You may think that all the teachings I share are just for you. I rejoice if you are blessed by our visits together … but the reality is … **I am sharing the truth God wants me to know.**

In 2 Timothy 3:7 in the Amplified Bible, God cautions us against:

> "... forever inquiring and getting information, but are never able to arrive at a recognition

and knowledge of the Truth."

It's not what you know ... **it's what you do with what you know that changes your financial destiny.**

If you don't like where you are in life right now with your financial situation ... chances are ... there's something you don't know yet!

I've made that statement in hundreds of cities, all fifty states, dozens of countries and to an international television audience ... pretty much on a daily basis ... but yet, some folks just don't get it.

Now let me quickly say that **I praise God for the folks who are getting it ... who've made a conscious decision to study ... to seek financial revelation ... to change the quality and direction of their lives.** I rejoice and Praise God over every testimony ... where the fruit remains, grows and reproduces.

Now I want you to listen very carefully to John 15:16 which says:

> *"Ye have not chosen me, but I have chosen you, and ordained you, that ye should go and* **bring forth fruit, and that your fruit should remain:** *that whatsoever ye shall ask of the Father in my name, he may give it you."*

When you are productive ... when you show yourself faithful ... when you study to show yourself approved

... when the fruit of your labors remains, the New Living Translation says that when we *"... produce lasting fruit ... the Father will give you whatever you ask for, using my name."*

Now that's what I call a good reason to study.

Day 17

7 Ways to Avoid Being a Prodigal

One of the first Bible stories I ever heard as a boy was about the Prodigal Son.

I find it interesting that the word *prodigal* isn't in most Bible translations, including the King James Version. The word is in the Amplified Bible, but it's not related to the story found in Luke 15:11-32.

In fact, the word *prodigal* according to dictionary.com was first used around 1500 A.D. Regardless of when the word was first used ... the definition of the word fits the son to whom it is now properly applied. It means:

"wastefully or recklessly extravagant."

I think it's fair to say that the Prodigal Son was wasteful. In fact, Luke 15:13 in the Amplified Bible says:

> *"And not many days after that, the younger son gathered up all that he had and journeyed into a distant country, and there he **wasted his fortune in reckless** and loose [from restraint] living."*

I find it interesting that most every Christian condemns this behavior saying (perhaps even sanctimoniously) that they would never have wasted their fortune in *"reckless and loose [from restraint] living."*

I feel prompted to ask several questions.

How much money has gone through your hands during your working career? Let's keep it simple. According to the Census Bureau, the median household income in 2011 was $50,054.15.

Let's say that members of the average household work twenty years ... that totals $1,001,083. If those household members work for 40 years the income is over $2 million dollars.

So, my question is simple ... what happened to the money?

The Message Bible translation of Luke 15:13 says:

> *"There, undisciplined and dissipated, he wasted everything he had."*

Let me just give you one example.

Once again, according to the Census Bureau, the average house price in America is $173,600. If you buy this house on a 30 year note at 5.5% interest and you only make the regular monthly payment of $985.65 each month ... you will have paid $181,245.41 in interest over the course of the loan.

You will have paid more in interest than the cost of the house. Would that be considered "undisciplined," or wasting everything you have?

I could go on ... to cars, credit cards ... department store cards ... boats, second homes, time shares ... but you and I would both grow weary of me calculating how much we've "wasted" in interest.

So, here's the question ... **what happened to the money God entrusted to us?** Would God consider our stewardship that of a prodigal son or daughter?

And by the way, I've been guilty. As Paul said, I'm the chiefest among sinners.

Let's not dwell on what we've done in the past except long enough to learn from it. **Stop and repent for having been a Prodigal.** I know I asked God to forgive me for being a Prodigal Son who has wasted money entrusted to me.

Now, zero in on what you're going to do from this day forward. **You can't change the past ... but you can definitely determine a better future.**

So, let's talk about the 7 Ways to Avoid Being a Prodigal.

1. Right Attitude

The Prodigal Son had the wrong attitude ... it was a me-me ... it's all about me attitude. Selfishness is a sin and certainly will never endear you to others or draw people with character into your life.

You need the right attitude.

Philippians 2:5 in the New Living Translation says:

> "You must have the same attitude that Christ Jesus had."

Now that you know the kind of attitude you're supposed to have ... how do you get it?

Ephesians 4:23 in the New Living Translation says:

> "Instead, let the Spirit renew your thoughts and attitudes."

2. Right Friends

The Prodigal Son didn't really have friends ... he had acquaintances who befriended him because of what he could do for them. When the money ran out so did they.

1 Corinthians 15:33 in the Amplified Bible says:

> "Do not be so deceived and misled! Evil companionships (communion, associations) corrupt and deprave good manners and morals and character."

By your words and actions ... you will draw like-

minded people into your life. Make a determined effort to choose friends who can encourage, exhort and edify you in your most Holy faith.

3. Right Timing

In 2 Samuel 11:1 the scripture says that at a time when kings went to war ... David tarried in Jerusalem. The next verse says that David walked out on the roof of his house and saw Bathsheba bathing. You know the rest of the story.

The root of David's sin ... was not the lust, the adultery or even the murder of Uriah, Bathsheba's husband ... he was simply out of God's timing. Had he been where he was supposed to be ... these sins would never have happened.

If you know God ... you will know His timing.

4. Right Place

If you're not where God wants you to be ... then you're in the wrong place and, most certainly, at the wrong time.

If we put ourselves in a place where sin prevails ... we're in the wrong place.

If the enemy is always tempting you with lust ... then stay away from television, movies and internet sites where sexual mischief and sin is continually on display.

Whatever the sin ... do not put yourself in the place where temptation grows into sinful action on your part.

What you feed grows ... what you starve dies. Stay away from wrong places.

5. Right Spending

The Prodigal Son made the wrong choices when it came to spending the money entrusted to him. I covered this in the opening paragraphs of this teaching.

As a reminder, the Message Bible translation of Luke 15:13 says:

> *"There, undisciplined and dissipated, he wasted everything he had."*

Right spending is ALWAYS spirit-led. **Never make major purchases without praying about it first.**

6. Right Lifestyle

It's really simple ... if you spend your money on everything other than how God has directed ... then you've chosen the wrong lifestyle.

Your personal choices ... your habits ... will either become your addictions ... or a testimony to you and the quality of your character.

1 John 2:16-17 in God's WORD Translation sums it

up when it says:

> "Not everything that the world offers—physical gratification, greed, and extravagant lifestyles—comes from the Father. It comes from the world, and the world and its evil desires are passing away. But the person who does what God wants lives forever."

Rather than choose the "Lifestyles of the Rich and Famous," why not choose "The Lifestyles of the Blessed and Born-Again"?

7. Right Thinking

<u>Is it time for you to have a Prodigal Son experience</u>? <u>Is it time for you to come to your senses</u>?

Luke 15:17 in the New Living Translation says:

> "When he finally came to his senses, he said to himself, 'At home even the hired servants have food enough to spare, and here I am dying of hunger!' "

When you come to your senses ... when you've been guilty of wrong thinking ... it's time for you to come to your Father. Luke 15:18-19 in the New Living Translation says:

> "I will go home to my father and say, 'Father, I have sinned against both heaven and you, and I am no longer worthy of being called your son.

Please take me on as a hired servant.' "

Great things happen when Prodigals repent for wrong thinking and sinful actions. Luke 15:20 in the New Living Translation says:

"So he returned home to his father. And while he was still a long way off, his father saw him coming. Filled with love and compassion, he ran to his son, embraced him, and kissed him."

You're welcomed with open arms ... and no matter what you've done ... you will hear the same words that were spoken in Luke 15:32 in the New Living Translation which says:

"We had to celebrate this happy day. For your brother was dead and has come back to life! He was lost, but now he is found!"

Now you get to choose.

Do you want to live in a ... **Wrong Attitude** ... **Friends** ... **Timing** ... **Place** ... **Spending** ... **Lifestyle** ... **Thinking** ...

Or are you willing to trust God for a ... **Right Attitude** ... **Friends** ... **Timing** ... **Place** ... **Spending** ... **Lifestyle** ... **Thinking** ...

Use It or Lose It

One of the most powerful men of God in modern day Church history was Dwight L. Moody.

Did you know he flunked church membership class twice in a row?

One time, after preaching, the deacon board called him to the side and corrected him, saying, **"Brother Moody, you massacre the queen's English."** (He was a very uneducated man.)

Brother Moody, about whom history records that, without mass media, he won over one million souls to the Lord, said to those who criticized his ignorant use of the English language, **"I'm doing the best I can with all I have right now. What are you doing with what you have?"**

Wow.

That's the real question for each of us this morning: **What are we doing with what we have?**

It's when you take what you have and **you give what you have to God** *right now* **that He's able to go**

into tomorrow and make provisions available for your next step.

Let me say that again.

It's when you take what you have and **you give what you have to God *right now*** that He's able to go **into tomorrow** and make provisions available for your next step.

In Matthew 25:14 … the parable of the talents ... the central question is, "What are you doing with what you have?" **You could say ... that it's use it … or lose it.**

Many have taken talent to signify one's natural gifts and acquired skills … clearly, the scripture is referring to money … however, as we study these verses you will see that the principles are the same whether you're talking about money or natural gifts or abilities.

Matthew 25:14-16 says this:

> "For the kingdom of heaven is as a man traveling into a far country, who called his own servants, and delivered unto them his goods. And unto one he gave five talents, to another two, and to another one; to every man according to his several ability; and straightway took his journey. Then he that had received the five talents went and traded with the same, and made them other five talents."

God is the author of increase? Let's continue in Verses 17-19 which say:

> "And likewise he that had received two, he also gained other two. But he that had received one went and digged in the earth, and hid his lord's money. After a long time the lord of those servants cometh, and reckoneth with them."

Now, the word *reckoneth* is an accounting term that means **"to balance the account."**

Verses 20-21 continue by saying:

> "And so he that had received five talents came and brought other five talents, saying, Lord, I have gained beside them five talents more. His lord said unto him, Well done, thou good and faithful servant: thou has been faithful over a few things, I will make thee ruler over many things: enter thou into the joy of thy lord."

I meet people all the time who hide their talents. They bury a part of themselves. They do not know how great it can be … how great they can be in the Kingdom of God.

To take any physical talent, spiritual gift or monetary resource and do nothing with it is truly an insult to God.

In Verse 21, God is also commending those who experience increase and multiplication.

God considers it a sign of spiritual health when we manifest increase in our lives.

Matthew goes on to say in Verses 22-26:

> "He also that had **received two talents came and said, Lord**, thou deliveredst unto me two talents: behold**, I have gained two other talents beside them**. His lord said unto him, Well done, good and faithful servant; thou has been faithful over a few things, I will make thee ruler over many things: enter thou into the joy of thy lord.

> "Then he which had received the one talent came and said, Lord, I knew thee that thou art an hard man, reaping where thou hast not sown, and gathering where thou hast not strawed: And I was afraid, and went and hid thy talent in the earth: lo, there thou hast that is thine. His lord answered and said unto him, Thou wicked and slothful servant …"

To take any physical talent, spiritual gift or monetary resource and do nothing is truly a shame. No wonder Jesus used the word "slothful."

Let's look at the seven characteristics of the slothful servant or seven things you never want to be.

1. ungrateful (Verse 18)
2. erroneous reasoning (Verses 18 and 24)
3. unjust (Verse 18)

4. fault finding; accusing (Verse 24)
5. self-justifying (Verse 24)
6. fearful (Verse 25)
7. wicked (Verse 26)

I want to point out a parallel of this story to our everyday life … **did you notice that the one who did the least did the most talking …**

Another point to consider, the words that any believer desires to hear is "enter into the joy of the Lord."

Here's the bottom line, **the Lord gave these three servants the opportunity to help build a better life for themselves, but one of them chose not to.**

What happened to him … let's look at Verse 30:

> *"And cast ye the unprofitable servant into outer darkness: there shall be weeping and gnashing of teeth."*

That's one place I never want to be.

The reason so many Christians never successfully complete the will of God is because they simply do not have an understanding of the kingdom of God.

The kingdom of God is governed primarily by the law of sowing and reaping, but we read here in Matthew 25 that the kingdom of God is also governed by a second principle that absolutely governs success in the kingdom of God. That principle is the principle of stewardship.

Stewardship is more than just money. It's everything. It's the total management of all the resources of God over which you and I have been placed to supervise.

As an effective steward **you have all you need right now to operate in His kingdom principles**.

What are you doing with what you've got right now? Because you have everything you need to obey God for today.

It's important to understand that God gives. In reality, God gives in seed form. The Bible says that God gives seed to the sower. A lot of what comes into our lives isn't harvest, it's seed.

Unfortunately, too many times God brings money into our hands and we think it's our harvest. If you need $100,000, and someone just gave you $1000, what you just got was your seed, not your harvest.

Deuteronomy 8:18 says:

> "But thou shalt remember the Lord thy God: for it is he that giveth thee the power to get wealth, that he may establish his covenant which he sware unto thy fathers, as it is this day."

The answer is in your hand. The answer is in your wallet. You have everything you need to do what God has told you to do for today.

Getting back to Matthew 25, the scripture we opened with. That scripture talked about the three stewards … the three managers.

Do you know who has to deal with the greatest temptation not to be an effective steward more than anybody else?

It's not the person with the much. It's the person with the little. It's the guy who had just the one talent. It's the person who just has the $100. **It's the person who has what they think is the little bit.**

What the third steward in Matthew 25 failed to see was that his obedience at his level would guarantee him a graduation at the level of the man with the 10 talents. It's our blindness to that graduation day that holds us back in our little bit.

What are you doing with what you have?

If you stood before God today, would He say, well done my good and faithful servant?

It's time to use it or lose it.

The Lost Art That Brings You Success

I was raised to demonstrate good manners.

Rudeness brought a sudden and swift response from my parents, especially my Dad.

I was taught that you take your hat (baseball cap or otherwise) off when you walk into someone's house.

You open the door for women ... regardless of whether they're your wife or your mother. In fact, if you're entering or leaving any building ... you should always watch out and hold the door for the person behind you.

You allow a woman to walk through a door before you.

You pull out a chair for a woman to be seated.

You thank someone for every single courtesy they afford you.

If a motorist pauses to allow you to cross an intersection or merge into traffic, you throw up your hand and say thank you.

If you're walking down the street with a woman ... you always walk on the sidewalk closest to the traffic.

You always put the toilet seat down when you finish.

You allow someone else to finish their sentence without butting in ... regardless of how valuable you feel your comments are.

If you sneeze or cough, you ALWAYS put your hand over your mouth.

If you're standing in a grocery or any other kind of line and a new lane opens up, you wait a few seconds and allow the people in front of you to go first.

You don't cuss in front of others ... as you might offend people who don't ... which also means you don't wear t-shirts with rude or vulgar sayings. I was raised that you don't do either.

You say "please" and "thank you" when you ask for something.

If someone says something you don't understand ... you say, "Excuse, would you say that again?" You never say, "Huh?"

If you're sharing a meal with someone, you don't start eating until your host is served or your host instructs you to begin.

You stand up if a woman or a senior citizen enters the room.

Don't ever comment on someone's personal appearance unless it's in a complimentary way. For instance, you don't say, "You looked tired."

Focus your attention on any visitor and not the TV or what you were surfing on the Internet.

If you're in a meeting and your cell phone rings, you walk outside the room to answer your call. Of course, it's best to put the phone on vibrate so you don't break the flow in the meeting.

Do not speak with food in your mouth.

You say, "Yes Sir or Ma'am," or, "No Sir or Ma'am," to anyone ten years older than you are.

If someone else sneezes, you always say, "God bless you," and offer them a tissue if you have one available. I will confess to you that I have politely asked a number of passengers on airplane flights to cover their mouths when they sneeze or cough.

That's 22 suggestions for good manners. There are more ... but this is a good start. If you or anyone else practices these 22 suggestions ... then the development of good manners in other areas will easily follow.

And in the words of H. Jackson Browne:

"Good manners sometimes means simply putting up with other people's bad manners."

<u>Good manners is more than just about being polite ... your manners shape who you are and how you value other people</u>.

Truthfully, I'm convinced that a lack of good manners is how we've lost the art of success.

But the question ... the real question is ... what does the Word of God say about good manners?

1 Corinthians 15:33 in the Amplified Bible says:

> *"Do not be so deceived and misled! Evil companionships (communion, associations) corrupt and deprave good manners and morals and character."*

If the scripture tells you not to be deceived and mislead ... then it means you can be.

You can know with absolute certainty that your Heavenly Father doesn't want you to be misled and/or deceived ... so the deception is from the enemy.

In a group setting, more often than not, conversation always goes to the lowest common denominator in the group. Rarely do group conversations rise to the highest level. This is especially true if the group includes someone who is rude and inconsiderate.

It's also worth noting that people with good manners sometimes allow what they've been taught and believe to take a back seat to the dominant influence of someone void of good manners, and if I may add ... void of common sense.

The scriptural admonition found in 1 Corinthians 15:33 is a very clear directive on who we should associate with and the standard of behavior that we're to exhibit and demonstrate.

If the scripture references manners of eating, then it must be important to God.

Proverbs 23:1 in the Message Bible says:

> *"When you go out to dinner with an influential person, mind your manners: Don't gobble your food, don't talk with your mouth full. And don't stuff yourself; bridle your appetite."*

There are some people ... notice I didn't say many ... who don't think table manners are important.

Here's what we know ... if something is important to God ... important enough to be included in the scripture ... then it needs to be important to us.

Some might say, well, I was never taught good table

manners, or manners in general, for that matter.

As I've always said, there is a difference between ignorance and stupidity. Ignorance is not knowing ... stupidity is not wanting to know or do.

If you've listened this far in this teaching ... then you're no longer ignorant.

Leviticus 20:22-24 says:

> "Ye shall therefore keep all my statutes, and all my judgments, and do them: that the land, whither I bring you to dwell therein, spue you not out. And ye shall not walk in the manners of the nation, which I cast out before you: for they committed all these things, and therefore I abhorred them. But I have said unto you, Ye shall inherit their land, and I will give it unto you to possess it, a land that floweth with milk and honey: I am the LORD your God, which have separated you from other people."

God actually finds bad manners disgusting. Any doubts? Check out the Contemporary English Version of Leviticus 20:22-24:

> "Obey my laws and teachings. Or else the land I am giving you will become sick of you and throw you out. The nations I am chasing out did these disgusting things, and I hated them for it, so don't follow their example. I am the LORD your God, and I have promised you

their land that is rich with milk and honey. I have chosen you to be different from other people."

If we want the best God has for us ... our own land flowing with milk and honey ... then we have to drop all excuses and learn good manners. God is telling us scripturally that He won't tolerate bad manners.

<u>It's my opinion that good manners define your character</u>. I was just blessed to be taught them early, but they're open to all who are willing to listen and learn.

If you're concerned about the welfare of others and how your actions appear and influence them ... then practice good manners.

Let's good one step further ... the demonstration of good manners speaks volumes about your character and morals.

Let's look at 1 Corinthians 15:33 again. It says:

> *"Be not deceived: evil communications corrupt good manners."*

In the Hebrew concordance of the King James Version of the Bible the word "manners" is defined as "morals, character."

Horace Mann said: "Manners easily and rapidly mature into morals."

Supreme Court Justice Clarence Thomas said:

"Good manners will open doors that the best education cannot."

We all need to understand that our mouths should be full of His Word, and that we must learn to say "please and thank you" ... if we want to be successful.

What To Do When You Don't Know What To Do

Day 20

"**I just don't know what to do next.**"

That's a statement I hear on an almost daily basis.

"I just don't know what to do next ... **I've lost the only job I ever had.**"

"I just don't know what to do next ... **if I don't catch up our past-due mortgage payments, they're going to foreclose on our house.**"

"I just don't know what to do next ... **our retirement income has been cut in half.**"

"I just don't know what to do next ... **my husband says he wants a divorce.**"

"I just don't know what to do next ... **the doctor says he's tried everything but nothing seems to be working.**"

"I just don't know what to do next ... **my son won't get a job; he lies around all day and parties all night.**"

Have you ever said or thought about saying: I just don't know what to do next?

The first thing you need to do is breathe a little deeper. You're not alone ... AND the good news is ... there is an answer.

How can I be so certain of that? The Word of God.

Jeremiah 33:2-3 in the New International Version says:

> *"This is what the LORD says, he who made the earth, the LORD who formed it and established it—the LORD is his name: 'Call to me and I will answer you and tell you great and unsearchable things you do not know.'"*

The Amplified Bible translation of Jeremiah 33:3 says:

> *"Call to Me and I will answer you and show you great and mighty things, fenced in and hidden, which you do not know (do not distinguish and recognize, have knowledge of and understand)."*

Elohim the Almighty One will show you ... things that you have no knowledge of. It doesn't matter whether you understand something now or not, because **God will show you "great and mighty things" which you previously had no knowledge of.**

The Message Bible translation of Jeremiah 33:3 is awe-inspiring:

> "... I'll tell you marvelous and wondrous things that you could never figure out on your own."

"Yes, but Brother Harold, does the Bible give specific financial advice?" If you're asking that question, then you've never read Ecclesiastes 11:2 in the New Living Translation:

> "But divide your investments among many places, for you do not know what risks might lie ahead."

This is excellent financial advice ... **I always counsel people to never put all their eggs in one basket.** There needs to be diversity in a person's investment portfolio.

For instance, figure out your basic living expenses on a monthly basis. This includes fixed payments (mortgage and car) as well as recurring expenses (food, gas, electricity).

<u>I recommend that you put at least three months of your basic living expenses into a money market account to which you can have ready access without penalty</u>.

Maximize contributions to an IRA account, 401K or other qualified plan. The tax consequences make these an important choice.

Based on your age and income needs, your investments should also include: precious metals, annuities, mutual funds, stocks, tax-free bonds and/or real estate.

There was a season of two years when we lived in Broken Arrow, Oklahoma, where I had the time to monitor the stock market on a daily basis. <u>I would buy and sell various stocks based on information that I learned from financial advisors who had a good track record</u>.

However, **the main ingredient in determining whether to buy or sell a stock was my peace factor.** I prayed for godly wisdom and the unction of the Holy Ghost to know when to buy and when to sell.

<u>Do I understand everything there is to know about investments</u>? No, I don't. **But I do know how to pray ... then I follow His leading about what advice is right and what is wrong**. My financial advisor is the Great I Am.

When it comes to investments ... you get a little different look at Ecclesiastes 11:2 by reading it in the New International Version which says:

> "Invest in seven ventures, yes, in eight; you do not know what disaster may come upon the land."

Both translations of this verse are making the same point ... **it's wise to diversify our investments.** Here's the bottom line ... the scripture gives us excellent advice on investments, but chances are it slides by way too many believers.

When you just don't know what to do ... go to the Word of God.

Jeremiah 33:3 in the New Living Translation confirms what I'm sharing with you:

> *"Ask me and I will tell you remarkable secrets you do not know about things to come."*

I continually marvel at advances in technology. I'm amazed at the lighting-quick speed with which you can find an answer to any question on the Internet. Just type in the keys words on Google Search ... hit the enter button and you have a wealth of information at your disposal.

However, there is a problem.

Have you ever noticed how you can find conflicting information on the same subject? Multiple writers or authors present information from their individual perspectives. You might agree or disagree with the thoughts being expressed.

Basically, the information you glean from a search on your computer was entered by a human ... so if the information is wrong ... it's because it was entered by someone based on their perception of the facts. In other words, **if you put "Garbage In" the computer ... then you're going to get "Garbage Out" of the computer.**

The mind of man is fallible ... but God is not! <u>Where we error is in not seeking the irrefutable truth to life's most difficult questions from the Word of God</u>.

Matthew 22:29 in the New International Version of the Bible says:

> *"Jesus replied, 'You are in error because you do not know the Scriptures or the power of God.' "*

There is only one source of information that is completely reliable ... yes, never wrong in its advice when you just don't know what to do.

2 Chronicles 20:12 in the Message Bible says:

> *"... We don't know what to do; we're looking to you."*

On more than one occasion I've encouraged myself with the words of 2 Corinthians 4:7-12 in the Message Bible which says:

> *"If you only look at us, you might well miss the brightness. We carry this precious Message around in the unadorned clay pots of our ordinary lives. That's to prevent anyone from con-*

fusing God's incomparable power with us. As it is, there's not much chance of that. You know for yourselves that we're not much to look at. We've been surrounded and battered by troubles, but we're not demoralized; we're not sure what to do, but we know that **God knows what to do;** *we've been spiritually terrorized, but God hasn't left our side; we've been thrown down, but we haven't broken ... While we're going through the worst, you're getting in on the best!"*

When you just don't know what to do ... get in the Word of God ... get in His presence until He begins to direct your path.

Proverbs 3:5-6 in the Message Bible says:

"Trust God from the bottom of your heart; don't try to figure out everything on your own. Listen for God's voice in everything you do, everywhere you go; he's the one who will keep you on track."

When you just don't know what to do next ... He always does.

Here are seven practical ideas of what to do when you don't know what to do next.

1. Decide anxiety, worry and fear are not the answers.
2. Get into His Word and in His presence.

3. Get your eyes off the problem.
4. Focus on what you can do next.
5. Do it now.
6. Recognize you're not alone in this battle.
7. Be flexible ... willing to change and adapt as circumstances change.

Remember this:

We may not understand the next step that God wants us to take, but God's Word says that He does. We can always **_trust in Him_**.

5 Ways To Get God's Help

If there is one thing that I desire ... it's to have such a relationship with my Heavenly Father that people will say to me what Abimelech said to Isaac in Genesis 21:22 in the New Living Translation.

> *"About this time, Abimelech came with Phicol, his army commander, to visit Abraham. 'God is obviously with you, helping you in everything you do,' Abimelech said."*

If you and I live our lives in such a way that "God is obviously" with us ... that's a powerful thought ... what a way to live.

Think what it means to have the Creator of Heaven and Earth helping us in everything we do.

The knowledge of His presence and His assistance should comfort and strengthen even the most insecure among us.

Here are 5 Ways to Get God's Help in Everything You Do:

1. Give to the Poor With a Willing Heart.

Deuteronomy 15:10 in the New Living Translation says:

> "Give generously to the poor, not grudgingly, **for the Lord your God will bless you in everything you do."**

There are three powerful points in this verse.

First, we're to give generously. That means it's not chump change or our leftovers.

Proverbs 11:24 says:

> "There is that scattereth, and yet increaseth; and there is that withholdeth more than is meet, but it tendeth to poverty."

The Contemporary English Version says:

> "... you can become rich by being generous or poor by being greedy."

How do you determine what giving generously means to you? It's simple. Ask God ... He will tell you.

Second, the scripture says we should not give grudgingly.

Deuteronomy 15:10 in the King James Version says:

> *"Thou shalt surely give him, and thine heart shall not be grieved when thou givest unto him: because that for this thing the Lord thy God shall bless thee in all thy works, and in all that thou puttest thine hand unto."*

This translation says that we should not be "grieved" in our giving, which is more often translated as "displeased."

Here's how to make God ... happy, happy, happy ... in our giving:

2 Corinthians 9:7 in the Amplified Bible says:

> *"Let each one [give] as he has made up his own mind and purposed in his heart, not reluctantly or sorrowfully or under compulsion, for God loves (He takes pleasure in, prizes above other things, and is unwilling to abandon or to do without) a cheerful (joyous, 'prompt to do it') giver [whose heart is in his giving]."*

The best way to never give grudgingly is to know that ... if God tells you to give, that's all the motivation you need. And always remember Ephesians 6:8 ... it's an attitude-changing, God-blessing scripture if there ever was one.

Third, the Lord your God will bless you in everything you do.

Now, even the thought of God blessing me in everything I do is a powerful, rich thought.

Deuteronomy 15:10 in the New International Version says:

> "Give generously to [him] and do so without a grudging heart; then because of this the LORD your God will **bless you in all your work and in everything you put your hand to.**"

The greatest thing about Deuteronomy 15:10 is that the verse doesn't say God "might" or "could" bless you ... it says He WILL bless you. That sounds like an absolute to me and fires up my most holy faith.

I rejoice that the Debt Free Army is helping orphanages in Mexico and Ghana. I also rejoice that we're helping to build water wells in India.

2. Don't Charge Interest to Fellow Believers.

Deuteronomy 23:20 in the New Living Translation says:

> "You may charge interest to foreigners, but you may not charge interest to Israelites, so that the Lord your God may bless you in everything you do in the land you are about to enter and occupy."

Why is this scripture so important? **God hates evil**

and debt is evil.

Psalm 97:10 says:

> "Ye that love the LORD, <u>hate</u> <u>evil</u>: he preserveth the souls of his saints; he delivereth them out of the hand of the wicked."

In reading this scripture, God showed me that debt is evil.

How can I make such a bold statement?

Consider the definition of the word *evil* as found in Strong's Concordance (H7451). It means **"bad, unpleasant, evil (giving pain, unhappiness, misery)."**

Debt is bad.

Debt is unpleasant.

Debt definitely gives pain.

Debt absolutely brings unhappiness.

Misery is a close friend of debt.

Therefore, as the scripture says ... *if we love God, we should hate debt.*

The scripture is also clear that **God hates financial slavery.**

Proverbs 22:7 in the Contemporary English Bible says:

> "The poor are ruled by the rich, and those who borrow are slaves of moneylenders."

I think this can help you understand a little better why God is so adamant about one believer not charging another believer interest. However, the scripture says if you loan money to someone outside the faith, you can charge them interest. That's an interesting thought.

Obedience to this scriptural directive is another example of how the Lord your God will bless you in everything you do.

I do believe if a person were to loan you money without interest ... you should bless them in some way for blessing you.

3. Obey His Instructions Even When It's Difficult.

When you're facing a tough adversary ... when the storms of life are swirling around you ... when it seems there is no way to make it ... that defeat is inevitable ... remember the words of Joshua 1:7 in the New Living Translation which says:

> "Be strong and very courageous. Be careful to obey all the instructions Moses gave you. Do not deviate from them, turning either to the

right or to the left. Then you will be successful in everything you do."

There is no conditional obedience to God's Word ... **you either obey it or you don't.** It's not a kinda, sorta thing. But obedience to His Word comes with immeasurable and never-ending benefits.

Deuteronomy 29:9 in the New Living Translation says:

> *"Therefore, obey the terms of this covenant so that **you will prosper in everything you do.**"*

4. Make Holiness Your Lifestyle.

Some think it's too difficult to live a life of holiness ... but **if the Word of God tells us that we must be holy, then it's definitely doable as a lifestyle.**

1 Peter 1:15 in the New Living Translation says:

> *"But now you must be holy in everything you do, just as God who chose you is holy."*

However, and it's a big HOWEVER, you can't do it on your own ... you must allow God to help you.

Psalm 37:5 in the New Living Translation says:

> *"Commit everything you do to the Lord. Trust him, and he will help you."*

5. Bring Glory and Honor to Him.

If you and I came with an owner's manual ... it would no doubt say that priority number one ... numero uno ... is for us to do what our Creator does.

We don't call the Bible an owner's manual, but that's essentially what it is for us.

Ephesians 5:1 in the New Living Translation says:

> "[Living in the Light] Imitate God, therefore, in everything you do, because you are his dear children."

On a daily basis you and I should desire that every step we take ... every word we speak ... bring glory and honor to Him. Our concern should be to represent His Godly character because we are His dear children.

1 Peter 4:11 in the New Living Translation says:

> "Do you have the gift of speaking? Then speak as though God himself were speaking through you. Do you have the gift of helping others? Do it with all the strength and energy that God supplies. Then everything you do will bring glory to God through Jesus Christ. All glory and power to him forever and ever! Amen."

A final thought ... God absolutely wants to bless us in everything we do ... but the choice is ours ...

What's Your Money Philosophy?

One of my favorite quotes is by Margaret Thatcher, the former Prime Minister of Great Britain who passed into glory in 2013. Baroness Thatcher said:

"No one would remember the Good Samaritan if he'd only had good intentions; he had money as well."

We remember the Good Samaritan ... not just by his good intentions but because he had money as well. **Money or the lack of money often affects our philosophy of life.**

Recently, the Lord allowed me to have a little **different look at the parable of the Good Samaritan**. There are **three very distinct "money philosophies" revealed in this story**.

Luke 10:30 says:

> "And Jesus answering said, A certain man went down from Jerusalem to Jericho, and fell among <u>thieves</u>, which stripped him of his

raiment, and wounded him, and departed, leaving him half dead."

The first money philosophy is: **What is yours is mine.**

The motivation of a thief could be evil, envy or error.

An evil man has a poor self-image without the benefit of a moral center. He will **take the path of least resistance**. He finds it **easier to lie, cheat and steal than to focus his energy in a positive manner**.

A heart without a moral compass has lost its way and views people with contempt. **Evil behavior is often passed down through generations.** However, the good news is that **one touch from God can turn even the darkest personality into one pure as snow**.

A heart filled with envy is never satisfied with what it has. It always wants what someone else has. These **are people who covet what their neighbors possess**.

There are also those thieves who **operate in error because they try to justify their sin**. This type mentality will **rationalize that they steal because they have no other alternative to survive.** This person will cite their lack of education or opportunity. **Situational ethics is a bogus philosophy. Sin is sin.**

The thief has the misguided money philosophy that "what's yours is mine."

Let's go a little further in our story. Luke 10:31-32 says:

> "And by chance there came down a certain priest that way: and when he saw him, he passed by on the other side. And likewise a Levite, when he was at the place, came and looked on him, and passed by on the other side."

The second money philosophy we see demonstrated is: what's mine is mine.

There are people who are **more likely to disregard the giving of their time and/or money to help or bless others than to help them.**

Sadly, some people **don't want to get involved in helping others because it's inconvenient**, **comes with a price** or perhaps **they just don't care. Neither of the three viewpoints line up with the Word of God.**

We have a **scriptural responsibility to help and care for those in need.** In fact, it shouldn't even be a question in our minds.

1 John 3:17 in the Amplified Bible says:

> "But if anyone has this world's goods

(resources for sustaining life) and sees his brother and fellow believer in need, yet closes his heart of compassion against him, how can the love of God live and remain in him?"

This whole **"what's mine is mine" attitude also reflects an attitude of shortage. This <u>person's limited thinking is centered on limited resources either in money or time</u>**, and <u>**they're unwilling to sow either of them into the life of someone else**</u>.

The fear is there **won't be enough time or money for what's on their own agenda.** In truth, <u>**this philosophy is one of self-indulgence**</u>.

<u>**The Good Samaritan displayed the third money philosophy: what's mine is yours**</u>.

Luke 10:33-35 says:

> "But a certain Samaritan, as he journeyed, came where he was: and when he saw him, he had compassion on him,
>
> "And went to him, and bound up his wounds, pouring in oil and wine, and set him on his own beast, and brought him to an inn, and took care of him.
>
> "And on the morrow when he departed, he took out two pence, and gave them to the host, and said unto him, Take care of him; and whatsoever thou spendest more, when I come

again, I will repay thee."

The Good Samaritan **recognized that all good gifts come from God** (Matthew 7:11). He also understood that when you bless someone in need, God will bless you.

Ephesians 6:8 in the New Living Translation says:

> *"Remember that the Lord will reward each one of us for the good we do ..."*

We're **admonished** throughout the scriptures to **develop a heart of compassion ... to love others with the love of God.**

2 Peter 1:7 in the Amplified Bible says:

> *"And in [exercising] godliness [develop] brotherly affection, and in [exercising] brotherly affection [develop] Christian love."*

The good news is that **developing and displaying Christian love brings its own reward.**

2 Peter 1:8 in the New Living Translation says:

> *"The more you grow like this, the more productive and useful you will be in your knowledge of our Lord Jesus Christ."*

However, it's important to consider some other things in the story of the Good Samaritan.

RichThoughts for Breakfast Volume 4

Luke 10:34 says:

> "And went to him, and bound up his wounds, pouring in oil and wine, and set him on his own beast, and brought him to an inn, and took care of him."

First, he went to him. The Good Samaritan chose to **make a conscious decision to get involved even though under normal circumstances it was unlikely the person would have given the Samaritan the time of day.**

Second, he "bound up his wounds, pouring in oil and wine ..." In that day, oil and wine weren't cheap ... they were **only carried by those who had financial resources.** So he was using something of value to care for this man.

Third, the Good Samaritan didn't just fix the man's wounds and leave him ... the scripture says that he "... set him on his own beast and brought him to an inn." The Samaritan walked to the nearest inn when he could have ridden.

The scripture doesn't indicate how long the walk was ... but I can tell you that it probably wasn't close. On two occasions, my fine wife, Bev, and I have traveled that road in a tour bus, and it is **still a desolate landscape ... who knows how much more in biblical times.**

Fourth, we don't know the purpose of the Good

Samaritan's journey. Perhaps he was on business ... but regardless **he set aside his own personal agenda to further care for this man.**

Do we hesitate to get involved in the lives of others ... to do something that's right **simply because it's an inconvenience to us and our daily routine?** That certainly was not the case of the Good Samaritan.

Fifth, the next morning the Good Samaritan paid the innkeeper for two month's lodging with a promise to cover any additional expenses. The Samaritan obviously had money, but he also **must have had a good name and respect.**

Finally, here's the question of the hour ... **if you were confronted with an opportunity to help someone in the same way as the Good Samaritan, would you have the heart and the funds to do it, or would you walk to the other side of the road?**

Sadly, there are those who are **unwilling to help others because they feel it might cost them too much. When you're in debt ... your ability to help others is limited, even if you feel the desire to do good things for them.**

Luke 10:36 says:

> "Which now of these three, thinkest thou, was neighbour unto him that fell among the thieves?"

There's a television commercial for an insurance company that says (paraphrased), **"Like a good neighbor, they are there."**

Are you free enough in your finances to be there when your neighbor has a need?

Does your financial situation determine your philosophy of life?

That's something to think about.

What It Takes To Be a VIP

Day 23

Have you ever been to an event where preferential treatment was given to VIPs?

Have you ever been told you were in a section reserved for VIPs?

Have you ever wished that you were a VIP?

Well, Child of God, I have a revelation for you.

YOU ARE A VIP!!!

Let's deal with the basic definition of a VIP. According to the American Heritage Dictionary, the term *VIP* is an abbreviation for *Very Important Person* and is defined as:

> **"A person of great importance or influence."**

According to Psalm 112:9 in the New Living Translation ... you are a person of influence.

> *"They share freely and give generously to those in need. Their good deeds will be*

remembered forever. They will have influence and honor."

The scripture is clear ... **the way to have influence and honor is to be a giver** ... that makes you a VIP.

However, I have another definition of what being a VIP really means in God's Word.

Value—How You See Yourself

Identity—Who You Are in Christ

Purpose—Why You Are Here on Planet Earth

First, let's deal with what the scripture has to say about your VALUE.

Without question, **you're valuable to God because He cared enough to send His only Son to die for your sins that you might have life and have it more abundantly**.

John 10:10 says:

> "... I am come that they might have life, and that they might have it more abundantly."

The New Living Translation of John 10:10 says:

> "... My purpose is to give them a rich and satisfying life."

Your value is forever established by the birth, crucifixion, death and resurrection of our Lord and Savior, Jesus Christ.

Philippians 3:8 in the New Living Translation says:

> "Yes, everything else is worthless when compared with the infinite **value** of knowing Christ Jesus my Lord. For his sake I have discarded everything else, counting it all as garbage, so that I could gain Christ."

Not only are you valuable to God ... but He knows everything about you.

Luke 12:7 says:

> "But even the very hairs of your head are all numbered. Fear not therefore: ye are of more **value** than many sparrows."

If you want to increase your value to God, then walk in obedience to His Word ... ever seeking His divine direction for your life. Proverbs 10:20 in the Amplified Bible says:

> "The tongues of those who are upright and in right standing with God are as choice silver; the minds of those who are wicked and out of harmony with God are of little **value**."

Even though you are valuable to God, it pays to continue to seek Him ... because His promises are obtained by your faith and not by your need. **As you honor His precepts ... you position yourself for greater protection and blessings.**

In Philippians 1:10 in the Amplified Bible ... the scripture tells us the kind of life that God wants us to lead.

> *"So that you may surely learn to sense what is vital, and approve and prize what is excellent and of real **value** [recognizing the highest and the best, and distinguishing the moral differences], and that you may be untainted and pure and unerring and blameless [so that with hearts sincere and certain and unsullied, you may approach] the day of Christ [not stumbling nor causing others to stumble]."*

Now that we've established your value to God ... it is nevertheless important to remember and realize that you will be held accountable on Judgment Day for your actions and reactions here on earth.

1 Corinthians 3:13 in the New Living Translation says:

> *"But on the judgment day, fire will reveal what kind of work each builder has done. The fire will show if a person's work has any **value**."*

The fact that you are a person of value is established in heaven and on the earth whether you realize it and walk in it ... or not.

Second, let's discover what the Word has to say about your identity ... who you are in Christ.

Romans 8:10 in the Amplified Bible says:

> "But if Christ lives in you, [then although] your [natural] body is dead by reason of sin and guilt, the spirit is alive because of [the] righteousness [that He imputes to you]."

Romans 8:11 in the Message Bible further clarifies your identity as a Child of the Most High God.

> "When God lives and breathes in you (and he does, as surely as he did in Jesus), you are delivered from that dead life. With his Spirit living in you, your body will be as alive as Christ's!"

1 Corinthians 1:31 in the Message Bible says:

> "... Everything that we have—right thinking and right living, a clean slate and a fresh start—comes from God by way of Jesus Christ ..."

Matthew 5:48 in the Message Bible says:

> "In a word, what I'm saying is, Grow up. You're kingdom subjects. Now live like it. Live out your God-created identity. Live generously and graciously toward others, the way God lives toward you."

Wow, are you seeing ... that you **have a God-created identity?**

Lastly, what does the Word have to say about your purpose?

Why are you here? What's your purpose on the earth? Make no mistake about it. God has a purpose for every individual's life.

Ecclesiastes 3:1 says:

> "To every thing there is a season, and a time to every purpose under the heaven."

If God's only purpose for saving you was to get you to heaven, then why not take you once you're saved? I mean, if our only purpose for getting saved is going to heaven, then load up the bus, and let's hit the highway to heaven.

Exodus 9:16 in the New Living Translation says:

> "But I have spared you for a **purpose**—to show you my power and to spread my fame throughout the earth."

You were saved to fulfill the Great Commission ... you were saved to obey the words of Mark 16:15-18 which say:

> "Go ye into all the world, and preach the gospel to every creature ... these signs shall follow

them that believe. In my name shall they cast out devils; they shall speak with new tongues ... they shall lay hands on the sick, and they shall recover."

It's also VERY IMPORTANT to fully understand God's purpose for our lives.

It is equally important that we see ourselves the way God sees us. <u>Regardless of our occupation ... He sees us doing the work of the ministry</u>.

Proverbs 1:3 in the New Living Translation says:

> "Their **purpose** is to teach people to live disciplined and successful lives, to help them do what is right, just, and fair."

You will fulfill your destiny not just because of your efforts ... but because of His desire as expressed in Psalm 57:2 in the New Living Translation:

> "I cry out to God Most High, to God who will fulfill his **purpose** for me."

No matter what circumstances, situations and problems you may be facing, they will not hinder God's purpose for your life.

Proverbs 19:21 in the New Living Translation says:

> "You can make many plans, but the Lord's **purpose** will prevail."

As I was writing this teaching, God revealed part of my purpose as expressed in Ephesians 6:22 in the New Living Translation:

> *"I have sent him to you for this very **purpose**— to let you know how we are doing and to encourage you."*

On this particular morning, I think the scripture clearly points out that **your VIP status is far more valuable than someone sitting in Reserved Seating at an athletic event or as a person who receives all the perks of being a celebrity.**

Let's see ... being a VIP in this world or being God's VIP? Oh, yeah, that's an easy choice.

Go to haroldherring.com and watch "God Can Use Even You." It's a two-minute video, and you need to share it with those you love ... actually, that's not true ... you need to share it with EVERYBODY.

God Won't Remember

Would you like for your Heavenly Father to come to your home ... at your current address ... in whatever city you live ... for a personal visit?

Would you like Him to sit down in your living room or at the kitchen table for a precious time of fellowship? Over the years my fine wife, Bev, and I made a lot of important decisions sitting around a kitchen table.

I could continue posing hypothetical scenarios for you ... but I think you've gotten the point ... or at least you're mentally prepared for what's coming next.

Do you realize that our great God Jehovah will do just that ... at any time and any place?

There is only one thing required for this divine visitation. PRAISE.

Psalm 22:3 says:

> "But thou art holy, O thou that inhabitest the praises of Israel."

Praise Him for Who He is ... what He's done for you ... what He's doing now and what He's going to do for you and those you love.

Not convinced that God is ready to sit down with you? Then let's look at the Hebrew meanings of three key words in the passage.

First, the word *inhabitest* is the Hebrew word **yashab** (H3427), and according to Strong's Concordance, it means:

<u>"to dwell, remain, sit, abide."</u>

Second, the word *praises* is the Hebrew word **těhillah** (H8416), and according to Strong's concordance, it means:

<u>"praise, song or hymn of praise; adoration, thanksgiving (paid to God); act of general or public praise."</u>

Finally, the word *Israel* is the Hebrew word **Yisra'el** (H3478), and according to Strong's Concordance, it means:

"God prevails" or "the name of the descendants and the nation of the descendants of Jacob."

To remove all doubt ... focus on Acts 3:25 in the Amplified Bible which says:

"You are the descendants (sons) of the

prophets and the heirs of the covenant which God made and gave to your forefathers, saying to Abraham, And in your Seed (Heir) shall all the families of the earth be blessed and benefited."

You can know with absolute scriptural documentation that God is always in your presence when you're lifting up His name in praise and thanksgiving. He clearly inhabits the praises of His people and that includes your praise.

Now believe it or not ... the purpose of this teaching is not to talk about Psalm 22:3, so you can consider everything up to this point as an appetizer as we move forward to the main scriptural course.

I was reading Zephaniah ... yes, that's right, Zephaniah. The book is located just after Habakkuk and right before Haggai. If you need more directions ... it starts on page 988 in my Bible, and yes, I'm smiling ... as I write that.

Here's the verse that I felt stirred to write about ...

Zephaniah 3:17 in the Amplified Bible says:

> *"The Lord your God is in the midst of you, a Mighty One, a Savior [Who saves]! He will rejoice over you with joy; He will rest [in silent satisfaction] and in His love He will be silent and **make no mention [of past sins, or even recall them];** He will exult over you with singing."*

The point I initially planned to make is that **God is in the midst of us because He loves His people.** And we personally know that God saves ... because He reached down and lifted us up from a life of sin.

But I must tell you ... **I thought it was kinda cool that God is rejoicing over each of us ... so much so that He's even singing about us.**

The King James Version says that God *"... will joy over thee with singing."*

The Contemporary English Version of that verse says: *"He celebrates and sings because of you, and he will refresh your life with his love."*

Having God singing over us ... is so much cooler than anything ever shown on *The Voice*, **American Idol or seen at any concert.**

However, that's not what stirred in my spirit as I read the verse in Zephaniah. It was the part of the scripture that says: ***"... and in His love He will be silent and make no mention [of past sins, or even recall them]."***

Right now, I'm going to expose one of the favorite tactics of the devil. He is continually bringing up your past sins and mistakes.

The enemy likes to remind you of the times that you may have joined in a dirty joke in front of your co-workers just trying to fit in.

The enemy likes to remind you of the time that <u>you didn't list all your income on your tax returns</u>.

The enemy likes to remind you of the <u>sexually inappropriate conversation, behaviors and actions you've had with co-workers or neighbors</u>.

The enemy likes to remind you of <u>the nights you stumbled into your home under the influence of anything but the Holy Spirit</u>.

The enemy likes to remind you of <u>foolish financial decisions you've made</u>.

The enemy likes to remind you <u>how you smart-mouthed the boss just before you got laid off the job</u>.

This kind of listing could go on for pages ... but the bottom line is this:

The enemy likes to remind you of your past sins even when God has forgiven them.

Regardless of what we've done ... God will forgive all our sins.

1 John 1:9 says:

> "If we confess our sins, he is faithful and just to forgive us our sins, and to cleanse us from all unrighteousness."

To be unrighteous ... as John says ... you must have

first been righteous ... so even if you've messed up after you were born again ... our loving Heavenly Father will forgive you.

The Amplified Bible translation of 1 John 1:9 says:

> "... will forgive our sins [dismiss our lawlessness] and [continuously] cleanse us from all unrighteousness [everything not in conformity to His will in purpose, thought, and action]."

Now if that isn't good news ... it gets even better ... **God not only forgives ... He forgets.**

Our dear friend, Bob Harrington, the Chaplain of Bourbon Street, likes to tell the story of how he woke up one night in a cold sweat from a really bad dream ... the R-rated kind.

Brother Bob said that he immediately slid out of bed onto his knees and started repenting before the Lord. His wife woke up and asked what He was doing. He told her he was repenting for a bad dream he just had.

She asked him to tell her about the dream so she could join him in the prayer of agreement.

As only he can tell it, Brother Bob said he told his wife that he'd handle the repenting. He said he knew God would forgive and forget ... but while she may forgive, he knew his wife would never forget.

The scriptures say "**... in His love He will be silent and make no mention [of past sins, or even recall them].**"

Need a little more scriptural proof?

Micah 7:19 says:

> *"He will turn again, he will have compassion upon us; he will subdue our iniquities; and thou wilt cast all their sins into the depths of the sea."*

Jeremiah 31:34 in the New Living Translation says:

> *"... And I will forgive their wickedness, and **I will never again remember their sins.**"*

Hebrews 8:12 in the New Living Translation says:

> *"And I will forgive their wickedness, and **I will never again remember their sins.**"*

The Message Bible translation of Isaiah 43:25 says:

> *"But I, yes I, am the one who takes care of your sins—that's what I do. I don't keep a list of your sins."*

How can God bring up your past sins ... if He doesn't remember them or even keep a list of them?

God will not bring up your past ... but the enemy will.

But he can only get away with it if you let him. That's why you have to forget the past and move forward.

Philippians 3:13-14 in the New King James Version says:

> "... forgetting those things which are behind and reaching forward to those things which are ahead, I press toward the goal for the prize of the upward call of God in Christ Jesus."

God will never determine your future based on your past, and we can all shout HALLELUJAH about that.

As you're praising God ... as He sits down to abide with you ... **you'll never have to worry about Him bringing up your past.**

Now that's something to shout about!

7 Reasons To Be Faithful With What You've Got

I want you to get hold of this next statement. Write it down ... get it embedded in your mental hard drive ... available for instant recall.

If I'm not faithful with what I've got ... that's all I'll ever get.

If we're not faithful where we are with what we've got ... we'll never arrive at any other destination than where we're at ... at the moment.

If we're not faithful where we are with what we've got ... it'll take more than Map Quest for us to ever find our way out of mediocrity.

If we're not faithful where we are with what we've got ... we'll never have to worry about our future success, because we'll never find it.

If we're not faithful where we are with what we've got ... we'll never hear God say, Well done My good and faithful servant.

If we're not faithful where we are with what we've got ... then He will never reveal to us secret riches and hidden treasures.

I frequently quote President Theodore Roosevelt who said:

"Do what you can, with what you have, where you are."

While that's a great quote by President Roosevelt ... I feel led to share with you seven reasons to be faithful with what you've got.

1. God is faithful, so He expects us to be faithful as well.

1 Corinthians 1:9 in the New Living Translation says:

"God will do this, for he is faithful to do what he says, and he has invited you into partnership with his Son, Jesus Christ our Lord."

If we're made in His image and after His likeness (Genesis 1:26), then we should be doing what He does. If He's faithful to do what He says ... then so should we.

2. Your intention to be faithful is a yes or no decision ... there is no if or if only.

Are you faithful? It's simple ... it's either yes or no.

Genesis 24:49 in the New Living Translation says:

> "So tell me—will you or won't you show unfailing love and faithfulness to my master? Please tell me yes or no, and then I'll know what to do next."

3. Being faithful is a choice.

Psalm 119:30 in the New Living Translation says:

> "I have chosen to be faithful; I have determined to live by your regulations."

Make no mistake about it ... being faithful is a choice, and God wants us to make the right choice.

He is even sending us messages ... just to make sure we get it.

Jeremiah 35:12-15 in the Message Bible says:

> "[Why Won't You Learn Your Lesson?] ... I have gone to a lot of trouble to get your attention, and you've ignored me. I sent prophet after prophet to you, all of them my servants, to tell you from early morning to late at night to change your life, make a clean break with your evil past and do what is right ..."

4. You are deemed faithful when you do what He desires.

1 Samuel 2:35 in the New Living Translation says:

> "Then I will raise up a faithful priest who will serve me and do what I desire. I will establish his family, and they will be priests to my anointed kings forever."

2 Kings 20:3 in the New Living Translation says:

> " 'Remember, O Lord, how I have always been faithful to you and have served you single-mindedly, always doing what pleases you.' Then he broke down and wept bitterly."

There must be a powerful thought in this verse ... something God wants us to get and understand, because the same verse is repeated again in Isaiah 38:3 in the New Living Translation where it says:

> " 'Remember, O Lord, how I have always been faithful to you and have served you single-mindedly, always doing what pleases you.' Then he broke down and wept bitterly."

5. You are recognized as a faithful person when you do what you have promised.

The best way to have an excellent reputation is to be known and spoken of as a person who keeps their word ... faithful to do what you've promised you'd do. I'm not saying that faithfulness to your word will always be easy ... it will not be.

Nehemiah 9:8 in the New Living Translation says:

> "When he had proved himself faithful, you made a covenant with him to give him and his descendants the land of the Canaanites, Hittites, Amorites, Perizzites, Jebusites, and Girgashites. And you have done what you promised, for you are always true to your word."

2 Chronicles 31:20-21 in the Amplified Bible says:

> "Hezekiah did this throughout all Judah, and he did what was good, right, and faithful before the Lord his God. And every work that he began in the service of the house of God, in keeping with the law and the commandments to seek his God [inquiring of and yearning for Him], he did with all his heart, and he prospered."

6. Being faithful in what you've got where you are ... should be a witness to others.

This point is really a follow-up to the fifth point. If you're recognized as a faithful person ... that will be a huge witness to every person who knows that you are a Child of God. You will be known for your faithfulness to God's work and His Word.

Ephesians 6:21 in the New Living Translation says:

> "[Final Greetings] To bring you up to date,

Tychicus will give you a full report about what I am doing and how I am getting along. He is a beloved brother and faithful helper in the Lord's work."

7. If you remain faithful even in the midst of adversity ... you will receive a reward.

It's comforting to know that your faithfulness is a major reason why He is willing to protect you against every attack of the enemy.

Acts 18:8-11 in the Message Bible says:

"In the course of listening to Paul, a great many Corinthians believed and were baptized. One night the Master spoke to Paul in a dream: 'Keep it up, and don't let anyone intimidate or silence you. No matter what happens, I'm with you and no one is going to be able to hurt you. You have no idea how many people I have on my side in this city.' That was all he needed to stick it out. He stayed another year and a half, faithfully teaching the Word of God to the Corinthians."

Nothing and no one can separate you from the love of God ... because of His faithfulness to you and your faithfulness to Him.

Revelation 2:10 in the New Living Translation says:

> "Don't be afraid of what you are about to suffer. The devil will throw some of you into prison to test you. You will suffer for ten days. But if you remain faithful even when facing death, I will give you the crown of life."

When you remain faithful you move into a deeper level of relationship.

1 John 2:24 in the New Living Translation says:

> "So you must remain faithful to what you have been taught from the beginning. If you do, you will remain in fellowship with the Son and with the Father."

When you're faithful to Him ... you always get what's coming to you ... and when He's the One bringing it on ... then you can know that you're going to be blessed.

2 John 1:8-9 in the Message Bible says:

> "And be very careful around them so you don't lose out on what we've worked so diligently in together; I want you to get every reward you have coming to you. Anyone who gets so progressive in his thinking that he walks out on the teaching of Christ, walks out on God. But whoever stays with the teaching, stays faithful to both the Father and the Son."

The Question God Wants Us To Answer

"I'm no good to you dead."

When I read those words ... I thought I was reading a script from a movie that I'd seen at some time in the past.

However, I wasn't Googling well-known Hollywood quotes ... instead I was reading Psalm 6:4-5 in the Message Bible which says:

> *"Break in, God, and break up this fight; if you love me at all, get me out of here. I'm no good to you dead, am I? I can't sing in your choir if I'm buried in some tomb!"*

The Living Bible Translation of Psalm 6:4-5 says:

> *"Come, O Lord, and make me well. In your kindness save me. For if I die, I cannot give you glory by praising you before my friends."*

I kept wondering why I was led to these two verses ... but I know that during my early morning time of prayer ... God always leads me to the things He wants me to see ... for a reason.

Truthfully, I was trying to figure out why God led me to these passages of scripture ... they had nothing to do with finances or success ... which is what He normally has me teach about.

Then the phone rang, and a good friend of mine was on the line. He runs an internationally known ministry and wanted my advice on a couple of matters, since I've done consulting in the past.

At the end of our 30-minute phone call ... he asked me to keep his wife in prayer because of some serious attacks on her health.

Next, he asked me to keep in prayer the wife of an award-winning recording artist and preacher friend of ours. According to the doctors ... his wife was terminally ill.

At that very moment I realized why God had led me to Psalm 6 ... I shared it with my friend who wrote chapter and verse and asked me to repeat the scripture in the various translations so he could write it down. He said, "That's just the word this woman needs!"

There are three lessons God taught me through this experience I've just shared with you.

First, while we may have a definite Bible-reading program ... we must be sure we are open to God's direction when He wants to change our course.

I take comfort in knowing that Romans 8:14 in the

New Living Translation says:

> "For all who are led by the Spirit of God are children of God."

Second, God always leads you to a passage of scripture for a purpose. Sometimes we may not know why ... immediately. It might be for our own personal edification or instruction ... but it could also be a word in season ... at the right time for someone else.

I'm reminded of 2 Corinthians 1:3-4 in the Message Bible:

> "All praise to the God and Father of our Master, Jesus the Messiah! Father of all mercy! God of all healing counsel! He comes alongside us when we go through hard times, and before you know it, he brings us alongside someone else who is going through hard times so that we can be there for that person just as God was there for us."

Third, you may be walking in divine health ... everyone close to you may be healthy from the top of their heads to the soles of their feet ... but God has a message for you in this teaching.

At first, I thought He wanted to me teach "I'm no good to you dead." But then He directed me to write and say that phrase over and over again.

"I'm no good to you dead."
"I'm no good to you dead."
"I'm no good to you dead."
"I'm no good to you dead."
"I'm no good to you dead."
"I'm no good to you dead."
"I'm no good to you dead."

Suddenly God gave me seven words ... that form a powerful question that He wants us to mediate on and answer. Here it is:

"What good are you to me alive?"

Wow ... "What good are you to me alive?"

Yes, we're no good to God dead ... but what good are we to Him alive?

Are we fulfilling His purpose for our lives?

Do we really know what His purpose is for our lives?

If not, have we asked Him to reveal our purpose for occupying space on planet earth?

James 1:5 in the New Living Translation says:

> "If you need wisdom, ask our generous God, and he will give it to you. He will not rebuke you for asking."

When was the last time you asked Him?

Are you doing the things God directs you to do in His Word?

Here are seven questions to help determine what good you are to God alive.

1. Are you winning the lost?

Acts 1:8 in the Amplified Bible says:

> "But you shall receive power (ability, efficiency, and might) when the Holy Spirit has come upon you, and you shall be My witnesses in Jerusalem and all Judea and Samaria and to the ends (the very bounds) of the earth."

Personalize this verse. Put your name in it.

> "But [Name] shall receive power (ability, efficiency, and might) when the Holy Spirit has come upon [Name], and [Name] shall be My witness in Jerusalem and all Judea and Samaria and to the ends (the very bounds) of the earth."

2. Are you funding the gospel and the Great Commission?

Matthew 28:19-20 in the Amplified Bible says:

> "Go then and make disciples of all the nations, baptizing them into the name of the Father and of the Son and of the Holy Spirit, teaching

them to observe everything that I have commanded you, and behold, I am with you all the days (perpetually, uniformly, and on every occasion), to the [very] close and consummation of the age. Amen (so let it be)."

Romans 10:15 in the Amplified Bible says:

"And how can men [be expected to] preach unless they are sent? As it is written, How beautiful are the feet of those who bring glad tidings! [How welcome is the coming of those who preach the good news of His good things!]"

3. Are you caring and providing for the widows and orphans?

James 1:27 says:

"Pure religion and undefiled before God and the Father is this, To visit the fatherless and widows in their affliction, and to keep himself unspotted from the world."

4. Are you giving generously to others so they will praise God for His provision?

2 Corinthians 9:10-11 in the Amplified Bible says:

"And [God] Who provides seed for the sower and bread for eating will also provide and multiply your [resources for] sowing and increase the fruits of your righteousness [which mani-

fests itself in active goodness, kindness, and charity]. Thus you will be enriched in all things and in every way, so that you can be generous, and [your generosity as it is] administered by us will bring forth thanksgiving to God."

5. Are you occupying anything other than the couch until He returns?

1 Corinthians 4:2 in the Amplified Bible says:

"Moreover, it is [essentially] required of stewards that a man should be found faithful [proving himself worthy of trust]."

6. Are you being successful in whatever your hands find to do?

1 Kings 2:3 which in the New Living Translation says:

"Observe the requirements of the Lord your God, and follow all his ways. Keep the decrees, commands, regulations, and laws written in the Law of Moses so that you will be successful in all you do and wherever you go."

7. What are you doing with the power to get wealth that He gave to you?

Luke 19:13 in the Contemporary English Version says:

"But before leaving, he called in ten servants

and gave each of them some money. He told them, 'Use this to earn more money until I get back.' "

Our answers to these seven questions have a direct bearing on the seven word question, "What Good Are You to Me Alive?" that He wants each of us to answer.

We are no good to Him dead, but we must each examine ourselves to determine ... what good we are to Him ... alive.

Praise God for testimonials:

A.S. from Texas wrote me an email several days ago that I would like to share.

She wrote: "Yesterday I sowed an online seed to your ministry. It was an amount the Lord had talked with me about, a very important seed to me and to Him. Today, I got three phone calls ... that resulted in $15,000 a month in contracts for my business."

Is God good ... or what?

7 Keys to an Immediate Breakthrough

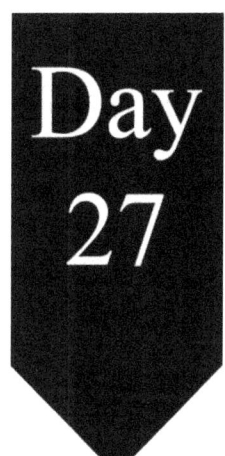

God wants you to know He can turn every situation around immediately.

No matter the adversity or how seemingly insurmountable the problem ... it's His desire for you to experience immediate breakthroughs.

Here are 7 keys to an immediate breakthrough.

1. Make an immediate decision to follow Jesus.

The greatest life-changing decision you'll ever make is to follow Jesus. Following Him will immediately turn you from a sinner to a saint.

Matthew 4:22 in the New International Version says:

> "And immediately they left the boat and their father and followed him."

Once you experience the immediate transition to eternal and abundant life ... you have a responsibility to tell others about the saving grace of Jesus.

Acts 9:20 in the New Living Translation says:

> "And immediately he began preaching about Jesus in the synagogues, saying, 'He is indeed the Son of God!' "

I'm not necessarily talking about a pulpit ministry ... but you are to become a testimony of what God has done for you to those who are in your circle of influence. Because if He did something for you ... He'll do it for everybody else.

And by the way, this just stirred me ... a decision to follow Jesus is much more than just accepting Him as your personal Savior. It's a decision to obey His Word.

2. When you reach out in faith ... healing virtue flows.

Luke 5:13 in the New International Version says:

> "Jesus reached out his hand and touched the man. 'I am willing,' he said. 'Be clean!' And immediately the leprosy left him."

The Greek word for touch is the same one used in Matthew 9:20 where the woman with the issue of blood touched the garment of Jesus.

When you and I read or hear the word *touch* we think of a light, gentle, faint tap with a finger or hand. Secular dictionaries confirm that definition.

However, it's not the definition of touched I found in the Strong's Concordance.

The Greek word for *touched* is **haptomai** and it means:

> "to fasten one's self to, adhere to, cling to."

If you want God to move in your finances ... it's going to take more than a light touch of faith ... you'll need to fasten, adhere and cling to His Word ... making it one with you.

Too many believers think that a light touch or momentary embrace of the Word is going to be a panacea ... or solve all their problems. Not necessarily so.

3. When you follow Him ... time, space and distance are of no consequence.

It's important to understand that when the scripture says immediately, it means right now.

According to Strong's Concordance the Greek word for *immediately* is **eutheōs** and it means:

> "straightway, immediately, forthwith."

According to dictionary.com *straightway* means "*at once*" and *forthwith* means "*without delay*." So it's fair to say that immediately literally means right now ... at this very moment.

John 6:21 in The Living Bible says:

> "Then they were willing to let him in, and immediately the boat was where they were going!"

God wants to do a quick work in and through you ... immediately.

4. When God directs you to do something ... don't delay ... do it right then.

If God directs you to pray for someone ... do it right then.

I've heard people say, "I'll pray for you," but walk away, and you hope they remember it later. If you're going to pray ... pray right now. Why wait?

God is ready to move anytime, anywhere. You can pray in the grocery store or in front of the gas pump as easily as you can pray by the side of your bed. God's still there.

Luke 4:39 in The Living Bible says:

> "Standing at her bedside he spoke to the fever, rebuking it, and immediately her temperature returned to normal, and she got up and prepared a meal for them!"

One more thing ... when God gives you an immediate breakthrough ... always immediately stop and give

Him the praise, glory, honor and recognition that He so richly deserves.

Deuteronomy 27:4-5, 7 in The Living Bible says:

> *"When you cross the Jordan ... take out boulders from the river bottom ... and build an altar there to the LORD your God ... and feast there with great joy before the LORD your God."*

5. Disobedience can bring immediate judgment.

Just as surely as you're blessed when you honor God ... there are consequences if you fail to give Him the glory He deserves.

Acts 12:23 says:

> *"And immediately the angel of the Lord smote him, because he gave not God the glory: and he was eaten of worms, and gave up the ghost."*

Likewise, when you and I fail to heed his instructions ... we may face dire consequences, so why take the chance?

We always like to talk about the benefits and rewards of serving God, but there is also a flip side to that equation. Our lack of obedience has its own consequences, and they're not the kind that you and I would desire.

6. Acknowledging God brings immediate manifestation even in seemingly impossible circumstances.

When you find yourself imprisoned ... and I'm not necessarily meaning incarceration with walls ... there is only one place to turn for your release from captivity.

Acts 16:26 says:

> "And suddenly there was a great earthquake, so that the foundations of the prison were shaken: and immediately all the doors were opened, and every one's bands were loosed."

Your deliverance is always preceded by praising, obeying and acknowledging God even in the most stressful of situations.

Acts 16:25 says:

> "And at midnight Paul and Silas prayed, and sang praises unto God: and the prisoners heard them."

Not only did the prisoners hear Paul and Silas, but so did God and the host of heaven. **The best way to break out of whatever is holding you captive is to look to God for divine instructions.** Praying and praising Him are the keys to breaking out of everything that has you bound.

7. Jesus will deliver you right now from every adversity.

In our lives ... we all face moments where we take our eyes off the Word and begin to look at our circumstances.

Peter did just that ... He was walking on the water until he starting observing the wind and the waves ... focusing on circumstances will make you sink just like Peter.

Matthew 14:31 says:

> *"And immediately Jesus stretched forth his hand, and caught him, and said unto him, O thou of little faith, wherefore didst thou doubt?"*

The very good news is that **God always has a grip on those He loves and those who love, honor and obey Him ... even though we may slip from time to time.**

There may be times in our lives when we're treated unfairly ... falsely accused ... left to feel all alone ... but we must never forget that we're never alone and that God can and will deliver us.

Many times Joseph faced terrible circumstances, but even when he was a slave, God was with him (Genesis 39:2, 4, 21-22). He may have been in bondage but his spirit was delivered and his heart and mind were at peace. Eventually, his inward faith was translated into an outward manifestation.

Genesis 41:14 in God's WORD Translation says:

> "Then Pharaoh sent for Joseph, and immediately he was brought from the prison. After he had shaved and changed his clothes, he came in front of Pharaoh."

We must always live our lives so that we're ready for immediate transition from where we are to where God wants us to be.

We must exercise our faith especially in moments when there is no visible solution to our problems. We must always remember that **God's greatest desire is to do an immediate work in all our lives ... so extend your faith with expectation.**

4 Reasons To Read the Instruction Manual

Have you ever tried to put together a swing set for your children and/or grandchildren?

Did you try to complete the installation without reading the instructions?

There are some things in my life that I NEVER want to do again, and one of those is putting together a swing set. There are fifty million pieces ... okay that's not really true; it just seems like there are fifty million pieces. Of course, everybody who's performed the task knows there are only a million pieces (just kidding).

I remember the first one I ever put together ... I tried doing so without reading the instruction manual ... big mistake. So after putting it together and then having to take it apart again ... I decided to read the instruction manual.

I became convinced the swing set instruction manual was written by a demon of confusion, and that swing sets themselves were created in the depths of Hades to test the ability of parents not to cuss.

Perhaps you've never had the swing set installation experience, but you've had a similar experience putting together toys for your children on Christmas Eve ... toys that had more moving parts than there were days in the coming new year.

I have discovered that instruction manuals ... while I may not understand them at first ... while I might complain because they just don't make sense ... while I'm frustrated over my inability to figure them out ... are valuable if I persevere. I soon realize that the instruction manual contains the answers I need. I find them helpful and much easier to understand than I had first thought.

<u>There are some folks ... who're not getting real answers to the real problems they're facing in life because they're trying to put their lives together without the benefit of their instruction manual</u>.

Some folks have decided the instruction manual for successful living is too difficult to read or understand, so they ignore it or only give it a casual glance in the midst of adversity.

Our manufacturer created an instruction manual for each of us to survive and thrive in any and every situation, circumstance and problem we face in life. However, here's a revelation ... if we don't read and study it, then we'll continually have problems all the days of our natural-born lives.

2 Timothy 3:16-17 says:

> "All scripture is given by inspiration of God, and is profitable for doctrine, for reproof, for correction, for instruction in righteousness: That the man of God may be perfect, thoroughly furnished unto all good works."

If something is profitable ... it's going to be beneficial. <u>The word *profitable* in the Strong's Concordance is from a Greek word that means "profitable, advantage</u>."

If we want to have advantages in life then we need to understand our instruction manual ... God's Holy Word. Every answer to every problem we face is in the book.

The Bible ... our instruction manual ... is an incredible tool for handling every single area of our lives ... and that most definitely includes money.

If we persevere in the Word, we can come up with the answers we need. And those efforts will far outweigh having to put our lives back together after we've messed them up through foolish financial decisions.

There are some who try to compartmentalize money into a secular rather than a spiritual category. You simply can't do that.

There are five times as many scriptures that deal with

money and possessions than there are that talk about heaven and hell.

Would it surprise you to know that there are almost twice as many scriptures on money and possessions as there are on faith, hope, love, healing and prayer combined?

That's an absolute fact.

God wants you to understand and activate every principle found in the manual so you can be financially successful.

The Amplified Bible translation of 2 Timothy 3:16-17 says:

> "Every Scripture is God-breathed (given by His inspiration) and profitable for instruction, for reproof and conviction of sin, for correction of error and discipline in obedience, [and] for training in righteousness (in holy living, in conformity to God's will in thought, purpose, and action), so that the man of God may be complete and proficient, well fitted and thoroughly equipped for every good work."

You should read the instruction manual because God wants you "complete and proficient" and fully prepared for every good work.

God wants you to understand money so you can be about kingdom business and not be hindered with the burden of debt and a life of financial insufficiency.

I'm going to say this again ... your financial life should not be treated separately or differently than your spiritual life ... as there is no distinction. The bottom line is this: How you treat money is also how you treat God.

God's instruction manual ... His Holy Word ... is designed to equip us for EVERY situation, problem, circumstance we face as well as the opportunities He sends our way.

The Word says that EVERY SCRIPTURE ... is profitable for our instruction. If you are not looking for revelation in the scriptures daily ... you are missing profitable instruction.

If you know that something is profitable to you ... it would seem that, without question, you'd do everything necessary to equip yourself with all the knowledge available to you in the instruction manual.

If you want to prosper ... walk in divine health ... run a successful business ... pray for your family and friends ... be delivered from addictive behavior ... get a seven-fold return on everything the enemy has taken from you ... manifest a 30, 60, 100-fold return on every seed you sow ... read the instruction manual.

Are you getting this?

Let me give you four reasons why you should read your Instruction Manual.

First, the manual will bring stability into your life regardless of what type of personal turbulence you may be experiencing.

Ephesians 4:14 in the Amplified Bible says:

> "So then, we may no longer be children, tossed [like ships] to and fro between chance gusts of teaching and wavering with every changing wind of doctrine, [the prey of] the cunning and cleverness of unscrupulous men, [gamblers engaged] in every shifting form of trickery in inventing errors to mislead."

Second, read the instruction manual because He said to.

1 Timothy 4:13 says:

> "Till I come, give attendance to reading, to exhortation, to doctrine."

If the Word of God ... our instruction manual ... tells us to do something ... then we JUST DO IT.

According to 1 Timothy 4:15 in the Message Bible we're not just to read the instruction manual ... we're to saturate ourselves in His Word.

> "Cultivate these things. Immerse yourself in

them. The people will all see you mature right before their eyes!"

Third, read the manual because truth builds upon truth.

2 Timothy 3:14-15 in the Amplified Bible says:

> "But as for you, continue to hold to the things that you have learned and of which you are convinced, knowing from whom you learned [them], and how from your childhood you have had a knowledge of and been acquainted with the sacred Writings, which are able to instruct you and give you the understanding for salvation which comes through faith in Christ Jesus [through the leaning of the entire human personality on God in Christ Jesus in absolute trust and confidence in His power, wisdom, and goodness]."

Finally, read the manual to understand the gifts that your Heavenly Father wants to give you.

1 Corinthians 12:1 says:

> "Now concerning spiritual gifts, brethren, I would not have you ignorant."

God does not want you ignorant about every blessing, benefit and gift that He has waiting for you ... other translations say that He does not want us "misinformed" or for us to "misunderstand" what

He's providing to us.

The only way you know what God's got in store for you ... is to read the instruction manual. Now, to me, that just seems like good common sense.

7 Reasons You Are Somebody

Way too many believers were raised in an environment where they were constantly told either directly or indirectly that they would never amount to anything.

Some believers even endure a marital relationship where they are demeaned and undervalued as a person ... and as a child of God.

Even more people just grow up not realizing that God has ordained them to be blessed and excel at everything they do.

Unfortunately, too many times our self-evaluation of who we are is determined by external factors based on inaccurate information.

<u>Who you are should never be determined by any basis other than the Word of God</u>.

Let me share with you seven reasons <u>why you are somebody</u>.

1. **You are the child of the Most High God.**

In contemporary jargon, *Who's Your Daddy?* God is!

Genesis 1:26 says:

> "And God said, Let us make man in our image, after our likeness: and let them have dominion over the fish of the sea, and over the fowl of the air, and over the cattle, and over all the earth, and over every creeping thing that creepeth upon the earth."

The Message Bible translation says:

> "God spoke: 'Let us make human beings in our image, make them reflecting our nature ...' "

You were created to be a master of the universe. The Living Bible translation of Genesis 1:26 says:

> "Then God said, 'Let us make a man—someone like ourselves, to be the master of all life upon the earth and in the skies and in the seas.' "

2. Your attitude of who you are ... should be continually changing for the better.

It's important that <u>your attitude changes from what others think of you to what God thinks of you</u>.

Ephesians 4:23-24 in the Amplified Bible says:

> "And be constantly renewed in the spirit of your

mind [having a fresh mental and spiritual attitude], And put on the new nature (the regenerate self) created in God's image, [Godlike] in true righteousness and holiness."

You are a work in progress ... continually evolving into what God wants you to be.

<u>When God looks at you ... He doesn't see limitation or hesitation</u>. When God looks at you, He sees the potential for creativity that He placed within you ... **He sees opportunities and possibilities.**

Ephesians 4:23, this time in the Living Bible, says:

> "Now your attitudes and thoughts must **all** be constantly changing for the better."

Romans 12:2 in the New Living Translation says:

> "... but let God transform you into a new person by changing the way you think ..."

Personalize this verse:

> "... but let God transform [Name] into a new person by changing the way [I] think ..."

3. **You are enrolled in a continuing education program because of who you are in Christ.**

Some people feel like once they've received their

high school or college diploma, that's it. They have arrived ... they're through studying. Nothing could be further from the truth ... life is a journey of wisdom.

Every day you and I should be striving to learn something that we didn't know yesterday.

Let me quickly point out that the "something" you are learning every day ... is not the latest scores on ESPN, the latest updates on the soaps or any other celebrity show.

Your continuing education should focus on what will improve the quality of your life while further fulfilling the destiny of who you are in the Kingdom of your Heavenly Father.

Colossians 3:10 in the Amplified Bible says:

> "And have clothed yourselves with the new [spiritual self], which is [ever in the process of being] renewed and remolded into [fuller and more perfect knowledge upon] knowledge after the image (the likeness) of Him Who created it."

I personally like the Living Bible translation of Colossians 3:10:

> "You are living a brand new kind of life that is continually learning more and more of what is right, and trying constantly to be more and more like Christ who created this new life within you."

4. You are somebody because of Him and not anything or anyone else.

<u>You are somebody ... because of who you are in Him ... not because of what you drive, where you live, where you work or anything else</u>.

Colossians 3:11 in The Living Bible says:

"In this new life one's nationality or race or education or social position is unimportant; such things mean nothing. Whether a person has Christ is what matters, and he is equally available to all."

As the scripture says in Acts 17:28 ... we are His offspring ... His children.

"For in him we live, and move, and have our being; as certain also of your own poets have said, For we are also his offspring."

5. You are somebody because He brings out the best in you.

Romans 12:2 in the Message Bible says:

"Don't become so well-adjusted to your culture that you fit into it without even thinking. Instead, fix your attention on God. You'll be changed from the inside out. Readily recognize what he wants from you, and quickly respond to it. Unlike the culture around you, always

dragging you down to its level of immaturity, God brings the best out of you, develops well-formed maturity in you."

Someone once said, "Change is a door that can only be opened from the inside."

Romans 12:1-2 in the Message Bible says:

*"So here's what I want you to do, God helping you: Take your everyday, ordinary life—your sleeping, eating, going-to-work, and walking-around life—and place it before God as an offering. Embracing what God does for you is the best thing you can do for him. Don't become so well-adjusted to your culture that you fit into it without even thinking. Instead, fix your attention on God. You'll be changed from the inside out. Readily recognize what he wants from you, and quickly respond to it. Unlike the culture around you, always dragging you down to its level of immaturity, **God brings the best out of you**, develops well-formed maturity in you."*

God brings the best out of each of us.

6. You are somebody with a special assignment.

You have a specific purpose, and God has a plan for your life. It's critically important that you discover what God has called you to do and be about His business.

Romans 12:6 in The Living Bible says:

> "God has given each of us the ability to do certain things well ..."

Personalize this: *"God has given [Name] the ability to do certain things well."*

Romans 15:14-16 in the Message Bible says:

> "Personally, I've been completely satisfied with who you are and what you are doing. You seem to me to be well-motivated and well-instructed, quite capable of guiding and advising one another. So, my dear friends, don't take my rather bold and blunt language as criticism. It's not criticism. I'm simply underlining how very much I need your help in carrying out this highly focused assignment God gave me ..."

7. You are somebody because you have the mind of Christ.

1 Corinthians 2:16 in the Amplified Bible says:

> "For who has known or understood the mind (the counsels and purposes) of the Lord so as to guide and instruct Him and give Him knowledge? But we have the mind of Christ (the Messiah) and do hold the thoughts (feelings and purposes) of His heart."

I also feel led to share The Living Bible translation of 1 Corinthians 2:16 with you.

> *"How could he? For certainly he has never been one to know the Lord's thoughts, or to discuss them with him, or to move the hands of God by prayer. But, strange as it seems, we Christians actually do have within us a portion of the very thoughts and mind of Christ."*

The truth of the matter ... we all need this last reason to know why we are somebody ... and no one ... can ever take that away from you.

Why don't you say it right now ... I Am Somebody ... I Am God's Body.

RichThoughts for Breakfast
Volume 4

Invite Harold Herring to speak at your church, event, or rally.

Would you like to invite Harold to be a guest speaker at your church, event, or rally? Just send an email to:

booking@haroldherring.com

or call 1-800-583-2963

With a mix of humor, practical strategies, and Biblical insight Harold will inspire, encourage, and prepare you to change your financial destiny and set you on the path to not only set you free from debt but keep you free of debt and living the debt free life God has called you to.

Keep Thinking Rich Thoughts,

Harold Herring

Join me each week!

This free email is something no one should be without. I guarantee you will be glad you signed up.

Harold Herring

RichThoughts Weekly Email

Weekly Videos

Practical Strategies

Biblical Insights

Thought Provoking Humor

These are just a few of the things you are missing if you're not signed up for the RichThoughts Weekly Email.

To sign up visit:
www.RichThoughts.org
and get ready to be inspired, encouraged, and entertained.

www.ingramcontent.com/pod-product-compliance
Lightning Source LLC
Chambersburg PA
CBHW061757110426
42742CB00012BB/1897